Poems

AND

A Defence of Ryme

SAMUEL DANIEL

From the title-page of " The Civil Wars " (1609)

SAMUEL DANIEL

Poems

AND

A Defence of Ryme

EDITED BY

ARTHUR COLBY SPRAGUE

Phoenix Books

THE UNIVERSITY OF CHICAGO PRESS

CHICAGO & LONDON

THE UNIVERSITY OF CHICAGO PRESS, CHICAGO & LONDON
THE UNIVERSITY OF TORONTO PRESS, TORONTO 5, CANADA

TO

HARRY SELLERS

PREFACE

SAMUEL DANIEL has something of a case against posterity. In a day when Elizabethan literature has sufficiently come into its own so that even its tertiary worthies may be read by those who wish to read them, he remains inaccessible. About forty-five years ago, indeed, the indefatigable Dr. Grosart brought out a *Complete Works in Verse and Prose*, but his five volumes are now hard to find — and expensive when found — and with readers of limited curiosity their very completeness is a drawback. A few of Daniel's works, *Delia*, for example, and the *Defence of Ryme*, have also appeared separately; but there has been no other collected edition since the early eighteenth century.

The need of an edition somewhat more carefully prepared than the last will be appreciated by anyone familiar with Grosart's want of pains in matters of detail. An extreme case is that of the sonnet beginning 'The onely bird,' which appeared in Newman's surreptitious edition (1591) but was not republished by Daniel. When Grosart came to print it, he gave the first four lines correctly, then turned two leaves and continued with line five of Sonnet XIII. Confronted by the ghost-poem which resulted, Fleay and Dr. Guggenheim could only suppose that Grosart was mistaken in affirming that 'The onely bird' had not been republished by the poet; and both said as much, pointing triumphantly to Sonnet XIII! Fleay had the further misfortune of relying on a Grosart variant reading to support his theory that Delia was Elizabeth Carey. It was noticeable, he thought, that while this lady was still unmarried Daniel called the river Avon, near which she then resided, 'rich in fame' (XLVIII, l. 11), changing 'rich' to 'poore' only in 1601 (*Anglia*, XI, 1888–89, p. 620). In reality, the change had been made seven years earlier while Delia was still 'a lamp of Virginity.'

The works reprinted in the present volume were chosen to represent Daniel at his best. The text is founded, *not* on the last editions published during the author's lifetime, but on the first. In defence of this departure from orthodoxy may be pleaded the unusual interest of Daniel's revisions — a subject touched on in the Introduction. In reprinting the first versions and collecting later readings at the end of the volume, I have considered the convenience of those who may care to see for themselves how an Elizabethan poet went about rewriting his verse. Other readers will perhaps be satisfied with an assurance that, although Daniel succeeded in improving many of his sonnets, *Rosamond* and *Musophilus* appear to the best advantage as he first printed them. The old spelling and punctuation have been retained; but long *s* is replaced throughout and a few palpable misprints, duly recorded, have been corrected.

To Mr. Harry Sellers of the British Museum, who knows much more about Daniel than I do, it is a pleasure to have this opportunity of expressing my gratitude for many acts of kindness. To signalize only two: he enabled me to collate a recently discovered *Delia and Rosamond* of 1598, just acquired by the Museum; and he placed at my disposal his own unpublished thesis on Daniel, which has been of help more than once during the writing of my introduction. I am indebted, also, to Mr. C. H. Pforzheimer of New York for allowing me to use his copy of the first (1592) edition of *Delia;* and to Professor G. L. Kittredge for advice and encouragement on many occasions.

ARTHUR COLBY SPRAGUE

HARVARD UNIVERSITY

AUTHOR'S NOTE TO PHOENIX EDITION

One or two corrections should be made in the Introduction. I am grateful to Mrs. Joan Rees for pointing out that Daniel's college was Magdalen Hall, not Magdalen; and, on page xiv, Grattan Flood's article has long been superseded by Mark Eccles, "Samuel Daniel in France and Italy," *Studies in Philology*, Volume XXXIV (1937).

A. C. S.

STRATFORD-ON-AVON

CONTENTS

INTRODUCTION

IN 1591, five years after Sidney's death, there appeared a small volume entitled 'Syr P. S. His Astrophel and Stella. Wherein the excellence of sweete Poesie is concluded.' Newman, the publisher, set it out with a characteristic preface by Tom Nash, and for padding appended 'sundry other rare Sonnets,' twenty-eight of them by Samuel Daniel, his first published poems. In *Delia*, entered in the *Stationers' Register* early the next year, Daniel referred to '*the indiscretion of a greedie Printer*' by whom his secrets were '*bewraide to the world, vncorrected*,' then republished all but five of the twenty-eight, this time carefully printed and, it would seem, carefully revised.

The accidental linking of his name with Sidney's was not unapt. At every turn Daniel had felt, and was long to feel, the influence of that Astrophel who had flown '*with the wings of his own fame, a higher pitch then the gross-sighted could discerne.*' Born in 1562, the son, says Fuller, of a '*master of Musick*,' he went to Oxford at nineteen. An entry in the Matriculation Registers, dated November 17, 1581, gives Somerset as his county — Fuller has him born 'not far from *Taunton*' — and Magdalen as his college. Seemingly, he left without taking a degree, and he was already 'late Student in Oxenforde' when his first book — a translation, at times Euphuistic in style, of a treatise on 'imprese' (or devices) by Paulus Jovius — was published in 1585. Soon afterwards, it appears, he travelled in Italy, perhaps with Sir Edward Dymock. In a commendatory sonnet attached to the latter's translation of *Il Pastor Fido* (1602), Daniel reminds him of how Guarini '*oft imbas'd/Vnto us both the vertues of the North*' and maintained that '*barbarous tongues*' could never bring forth poetry; and in *Delia* two sonnets refer to an Italian journey, one of them, the forty-fourth, in 1592.* At what time he began to enjoy the favor of the Pembrokes of Wilton is uncertain. In the *Defence of Ryme* he speaks of having been 'first incourag'd or fram'd' to the writing of verse by Sidney's sister — that Mary, Countess of Pembroke, whose name recurs in Daniel's writings, and always, I think, with unaffected respect and attachment. It was at Wilton, rich in its associations with Sidney and the *Arcadia*, that he received 'the first notion for the formall ordering of those compositions'; and 'afterward, drawne farther on by the well-liking and approbation of my worthy Lord,' William Herbert, Mary's son, he 'aduentured to bestow all his whole powers therein.' Wilton was his 'best Schoole,' whereof he would ever 'hold a feeling and gratefull Memory.' There, too, it is likely, he met that indubitable if perverse genius, Fulke Greville, Sidney's friend and biographer. The recently recovered original conclusion to the *Musophilus* is in itself enough to show how powerful an influence Greville exerted over Daniel's early fortunes.†

* For another Daniel, who also travelled and who has been confused with the poet, see W. H. Grattan Flood's article, 'Was Samuel Daniel in France in 1584–1586?,' *Review of English Studies*, 1926, pp. 98–99.

† Lines 995 ff. The passage was first reprinted by Mr. Sellers, *Modern Language Review*, January, 1916. Greville has been more or less tradi-

Who, all this while, was the reluctant Delia of the sonnets? The older critics, Fleay for instance and Grosart, set so much store by her, the poet gives them so little to work on! She lived on the Avon (probably the Wiltshire, not the Stratford, Avon); while other beauties came to London she was 'left to adorne the West': that is all. If one *had* to say who she was, it would be the Countess of Pembroke. Sidney's sister would have understood how the sonnets were to be taken; and there is a good deal in the tone of them, in the dedication-like recurrence of the Delia theme in the *Rosamond*, to suggest the celebration of a patron rather than that of a mistress. As it happens, however, the one seeming clue leads nowhere. Thus the sonnet, 'Like as the spotlesse *Ermelin*,' which appears in only the second of the two editions of 1592, is headed 'To *M.P.*,' and in *The Civil Wars* (VIII, 76) Daniel's Countess is plain '*Mary Pembrooke*.' Also, the initials 'M.P.' are stamped on some of her books, including a copy of *Delia and Rosamond* now in the Widener collection. But '*M.P.*' may refer to another person, a man mentioned in the introductory letter to *Paulus Jovius*, — a friend of the writer's, whom Daniel knew. And again, if 'Mary Pembrooke' is Delia right through, why should this one sonnet be signalized? Perhaps it is as well to go no further. If one takes Delia too literally, one has to determine why her lover, having spoken of his 'three yeeres

tionally identified as the learned gentleman with whom Daniel corresponded on matters of prosody not long before the publication of the *Defence of Ryme* (see p. 127, below); and Mr. Sellers has unearthed a letter of Greville's which shows that he was looking for an Isle of Wight parsonage for Daniel in 1595 (*Hist. MSS. Comm. Reports*, Hatfield House, part v, 1894, p. 166).

witnes' in 1592 (xxvi, l. 6), should in revising the
line in 1601 change the 'three' to only 'fiue'; and,
what is even more exacting, has to explain why
her hair was 'golden' in 1592, 'sable' in 1601 (xxxiii,
14; xxxiiii, 1). And at this point the modern
scholars, with Sir Sidney Lee (very angry) at their
head, demand a hearing. Daniel's sonnets were at
first merely in the Petrarchan tradition, with some
particular obligations to Tasso. But the sum of his
liabilities has mounted steadily, with French authors
like Du Bellay and Desportes assuming prominence
in the account, till at last one finds the learned judges
agreeing that the culprit is guilty of egregious thefts,
and only falling foul of one another as to the identity
of some of the victims.* Through their exertions
they have at least disposed of the autobiographical
incubus, and one may still enjoy the sonnets as sonnets.

Most of them are in the English, or Shakespearean
form, with three quatrains and a final couplet. Lack-
ing, as a rule, the surge and lift of which the form is
capable, they offer instead purity of diction, tranquil
but by no means drowsy rhythms, and the perfection
of single lines.

O cleer-eyde Rector of the holie Hill,

* Compare Josef Guggenheim, *Quellenstudien zu Samuel Daniels
Sonettencyklus „Delia,"* Berlin [1898]; Lee, Preface to *Elizabethan Sonnets,
French Renaissance in England* and *Life of Shakespeare;* the articles of
Kastner and Ruutz-Rees in *Modern Language Review,* 1907–08, 1912,
and *Modern Language Notes,* 1909; and, for a sensible recapitulation, G.
K. Brady, *Samuel Daniel,* Urbana, Illinois, 1923. The list does not pre-
tend to be exhaustive.

and

> A modest maide, deckt with a blush of honour,
> Whose feete doe treade greene pathes of youth and loue,

have been underscored again and again; and, if whole
poems are wanted, there are those in the *Oxford Book*
— and one's own favorites. On the question of their
alleged plagiarism, finally, there is a word more to
say, and it has been well said by Professor Elton.
'We talk,' he writes in his *Michael Drayton*, 'of the
debts of this man to that; but in such a case the credi-
tor is a messenger rather than a giver. And every
such debt is a challenge to original power of treat-
ment, and is cancelled if that be forthcoming. Treat-
ment is all; but the power to treat depends on the
poet's soul and experience.'

The Complaint of Rosamond belongs in time and
spirit with *Delia*, its companion-piece. Back of it lies
the ponderous *Mirror for Magistrates*, with its 'chain-
gang of illustrious victims' fallen from greatness; and
Daniel himself recognized the consanguinity between
his heroine and 'Shore's wife,' the well-told tale of
whom had first appeared in the *Mirror* thirty years
before. So, too, did old Churchyard recognize it, the
author, who only waited for the success of *Rosamond*
('so excellently sette forth' it was!) to bring out a
new edition of his own tale — 'not in any kind of emulation,' of course, 'but to make the world knowe his
device in age was as ripe and reddie as his disposition
and knowledge was in youth.' To set the two poems
side by side is to become conscious of the wonder-
working advances of those thirty years. Both are in

the seven-line stanza of the *Troilus* and Sackville's *Induction*. They tell similar stories of royal mistresses, are alike in their mingling of narration and moralization, their set speeches and sententious couplets. But *Shore's Wife* seems stiff and archaic today; while *Rosamond* at its best—in the lament of King Henry, for instance, and the loveliness of single verses like

Thys sorrowing farewell of a dying kisse —

suggests Marlowe and the Ovidians.* It is, also, a Clifford poem; and in an age when patronage counted for so much in the lives of poets the Cliffords may not go quite unmentioned. To Margaret, Countess of Cumberland, a courageous woman ill used by her husband, George the third Earl, and after his death harassed by litigation, Daniel dedicated his *Letter from Octavia to Marcus Antonius* (an inferior *Rosamond*) in 1599. Probably about that time he became tutor to Margaret's daughter, Lady Anne Clifford, who years afterward erected a monument to him in Beckington Church.†

Delia and *Rosamond* were followed by *Cleopatra* in 1594, and by *The First Fowre Bookes of the ciuile warres betweene the two houses of Lancaster and Yorke* in 1595. *Cleopatra*, written to accompany the Countess

* Both *Delia* and *Rosamond* are held to have influenced Shakespeare, — *Delia* least doubtfully, perhaps, in its use of the English sonnet-form and the changes it rings on the theme of poetical immortality. Daniel has even been thrust forward with Chapman, Jonson, and Barnabe Barnes (God save the mark!) as 'the rival poet.'

† The well-known letter to Egerton in which Daniel is represented as complaining that, 'whilst he should haue written the actions of *men*, he had been constrayned to liue with *children*' is now suspected to be another Collier forgery. Its rehabilitation is not to be desired.

of Pembroke's *Antonie*, is a strictly formed Senecan tragedy in alternate rhyme. It has a chorus, 'all Egyptians,' and the action is limited to the events subsequent to Antony's death. With the achievements of Shakespeare and the romantic dramatists in mind, it is only too easy at once to deride the play as a play and to overlook its virtues as literature. After all, it bears reading surprisingly well. *The Civil Wars* mounted, in the course of years, to eight books and about seven thousand ottava-rima lines; and yet Daniel, who began with the second Richard and proposed to conclude with '*the glorious Vnion of* Hen. *7*,' had at last only reached Edward the Fourth and his marriage with the Lady Grey. Like many another ambitious project of the time, it was, indeed, a mistake from the outset. Daniel would 'versifie the troth, not Poetize'; trusting that what he wrote would prove '*a gratefull worke to his Countrie*,' he did not consider too closely '*what weapon of vtterance*' he was using. The result, as his contemporaries perceived, was verse-chronicle, not epic. And Ben Jonson, whose relations with him were none of the friendliest, pitched upon a further weakness, remarking to Drummond that 'Daniel wrott Civill Warres, and yett hath not one batle in all his book' — a charge which Grosart took quite literally and tried to confute.

Daniel had been cheered on to write *The Civil Wars* by Charles Blount, Lord Mountjoy. To this grave nobleman, who had fought beside Sidney at Zutphen and who succeeded him as the lover of Penelope Devereux (Lady Rich), Daniel dedicated his *Poeticall*

Essayes, a volume of collected verse, in 1599. 'This I do,' he wrote,

> to th'end if destinie
> Shall any monument reserue of me,
> Those times should see my loue, how willing I
> That liu'd by thee, would haue thee liue with me.*

The volume contains, besides *Cleopatra*, *Civil Wars*, *Delia*, and *Rosamond*, the dismal *Letter from Octavia*, and one of the best, certainly the most characteristic, of his poems, *Musophilus*. To this last work it will be necessary to return when Daniel's writings are re-viewed as a whole. Meanwhile, it is a verse-dialogue in which Philocosmus, the unlettered man of action, is opposed by the defender of culture, 'of all *learn-ing*,' Musophilus. There is no direct source — it pre-sents *'the forme of mine owne heart,'* wrote the poet; but Courthope is right in associating it with Castiglione's *Courtier*. In that graceful treatise on Renaissance ideals, the French are charged with a heresy akin to the heresy of Philocosmus: they 'know onely the noblenes of armes, and passe for nothing beside: so that they doe not onely set by letters, but they rather abhorre them, and all learned men they doe count very rascalles.' Whereupon Count Ludovico, speak-ing for the author, is so anxious to have a tilt with them — 'or with other that were of a contrary opinion to him' — that he cannot forbear giving a few heads of an answer showing that letters are 'profitable and necessarie for our life and estimation.' On this sub-

---

* Compare *A Funerall Poeme Vppon the Death of the late noble Earle of Deuonshyre*, and *Civil Wars*, book I, stanza 5 (except in the case of items reprinted in the present volume, all Daniel references are to Grosart's edition).

ject, however, he is so far from finding an opponent that good old Pietro Bembo is moved to ask why the ideal courtier of their framing, 'being learned, and of so many other vertuous qualities,' should 'count every thing for an ornament of armes, and not armes, and the rest for an ornament of letters.' * There the matter rested.

That much in Daniel's poem had long been pondered over before receiving full expression is plain to any one who has read the Dedication of his *Cleopatra* to the Countess of Pembroke. In it he speaks, for example, of the many pens levelled like spears against that

> tyrant of the North;
> *Grosse Barbarisme*, whose powre grown far inlarg'd
> Was lately by thy valiant brothers worth
> First found, encountred, and prouoked forth. . . .
>
> And now must I with that poore strength I haue,
> Resist so foule a foe in what I may:
> And arme against Obliuion and the Graue,
> That else in darkenesse carries all away,
> And makes of all an vniuersall pray.

Then, turning to the narrow limits within which the literature of England is confined, he sighs for the coming of a poet great enough to break down those limits, so that '*Tyber*, *Arne*, and *Po*' may hear 'how far Thames doth out-go/The Musike of declined *Italy*.'

In 1603 James came to the throne, and Daniel commenced courtier with a *Panegyrike Congratulatorie*, in which he mingled his own high hopes of good days to come, under a learned monarch, with advice, tactfully

* *Il Cortegiano*, ed. Vittorio Cian, Firenze, 1910, pp. 106–112. The quotations are from Hoby's translation, which I think Daniel knew.

offered, as to how the learned monarch was to behave. The same year saw the publication of *Epistles* and *A Defence of Ryme*. In their seasoned thought and noble expression the *Epistles* are characteristic poems of Daniel's maturity. Curiously enough, the three to women are better than the three to men. They are the Epistle to that gracious friend of poets, Lucy, Countess of Bedford; that to Anne Clifford, with the hushed beauty of its opening,

> Vnto the tender youth of those faire eyes
> The light of iudgement can arise but new,
> And yong the world appeares t'a yong conceit;

and, best of all, the Epistle to Lady Margaret of which Quiller-Couch once wrote, 'Certainly, if ever a critic shall arise to deny poetry the virtue we so commonly claim for her, of fortifying men's souls against calamity, this noble Epistle will be all but the last post from which he will extrude her defenders.' *

The *Defence of Ryme* was provoked by an aberration of Thomas Campion, the lyrist, who in 1602 took it upon himself to publish a frothy little pamphlet called *Observations in the Art of English Poesie*. It is hard, at this distance, to tell just what Campion was about. His was not, plainly, the old quarrel of the Areopagus group, contending for a strictly classical prosody. Their dactyls, he saw, would not do in English, and the attempts to acclimatize them had met 'with passing pitifull successe.' 'The accent,' moreover was 'diligently to be obseru'd, for chiefly by the accent in any language the true value of the sillables

* *Adventures in Criticism*, 'Samuel Daniel.'

is to be measured.' So far so good. But 'the next rule is position, which makes euery sillable long, whether the position happens in one or in two words, according to the manner of the *Latines*'; and he passes, accordingly to 'the censure of our sillables.' For though, 'if we examine our owne writers, we shall find they vnawares hit oftentimes vpon the true *Iambick* numbers,' it is by ear alone and not 'the guidance of arte.' But especially he attacks 'the childish titillation' of rhyming, offspring of those 'lack-learning times' after the decline of Rome, and the chief cause, doubtless, of that prosodic chaos he had set out to reform. In answering Campion, Daniel appeals to Custom and Nature — 'Custome that is before all Law, Nature that is aboue all Arte.' His specific arguments for the use of rhyme are cogent even today. It gives 'to the Eare an Eccho of a delightfull report & to the Memorie a deeper impression.' It is a jointure without which verse is only too apt to run 'wildely on, like a tedious fancie without a close.' Rhyme is no impediment to 'an eminent spirit whome Nature hath fitted for that mysterie': rather it 'giues him wings to mount and carries him, not out of his course, but as it were beyond his power to a farre happier flight.' The *Defence* is, in truth, much more than a refutation of Campion. It is a Magna Charta against arrogance and affectation. An historical sense which has brought the author to a realization of the nature of human progress is combined, in its pages, with his love of England and of England's past. 'Me thinkes,' he writes, 'we should not so soone yeeld our consents captiue to the authoritie of Antiquitie, vnlesse we

(xxiii)

saw more reason: all our vnderstandings are not to be built by the square of *Greece* and *Italie*. We are the children of nature as well as they.' In an age when controversial writing was almost certain to resolve itself into vituperation, he meets his opponent with perfect courtesy; with the recognition, indeed, that since, 'next to the awe of heauen, the best reine, the strongst hand to make men keepe their way, is that which their enemy beares vpon them,' opposition is in itself healthful. His style, lastly, is of singular propriety and grace. Ben told Drummond 'he had written a Discourse of Poesie both against Campion and Daniel, especially this last.' Whatever may have been the merits of his lost treatise, it was almost certainly inferior, as prose, to *A Defence of Ryme*.

The *Panegyrike Congratulatorie* was a bid for preferment which did not pass unheeded. Daniel was commissioned to write a masque, *The Vision of the Twelve Goddesses*, for the new king's first Christmas at Hampton Court; and early in 1604 he was appointed licenser for the Children of the Queen's Revels, who were to give no play without his approbation and allowance. I can find little to praise in *The Twelve Goddesses*, which will not compare for a moment with Jonson's early masques. Elizabeth's wardrobe was pillaged for the costumes worn by Anne and her ladies as the Goddesses. Sidney's 'Stella' (Lady Rich) appeared, as Venus, 'in a Mantle of Doue-colour, and siluer, imbrodred with Doues' and 'a Skarffe of diuers colours.' Lucy, Countess of Bedford, a prime mover, it would seem, in the whole enterprise, was Vesta, and the new queen, Pallas. Dudley Carleton, a contemporary letterwriter, says that 'theyr heads by theyr dressing did onely distinguish the difference of yᵉ Goddesses they did represent' — which shows that he was not attending too closely. 'Onely Pallas,' he adds guilelessly, 'had a trick by herself, for her clothes were not so much below the knee but that we might see a woeman had both feete and legs which I never knew before.' * Daniel's initial relations with the patentees of the Queen's Revels yielded him a bond of £100. and an annuity of £10.; but these he made over to another on April 28, 1605, and thenceforward 'neaver intermedled or had to doe' with the company. His retirement may have been brought about by the unfortunate reception of *Philotas*, his second tragedy, on its production the autumn before.†

Philotas, which in form resembles *Cleopatra*, is founded on the story of Alexander's favorite as recounted by Plutarch. It was held to resemble the late Essex conspiracy too nearly, and Daniel was haled before the lords in council to satisfy them of its innocence. This he succeeded in doing. He had written the first three acts, he told them, 'the Christmas before my L. of Essex troubles, as diuers in the cittie could witnes.' The resemblances were so many coincidences; for 'there is nothing new vnder the Sunne, nothing in theas tymes yᵗ is not in bookes, nor in bookes that is not in theas tymes.' The play, he said,

---

* *The Vision of the Twelve Goddesses*, ed. Ernest Law, 1880, pp. 43, 45. This dainty reprint by the Chiswick Press is still to be picked up at very small cost.

† R. E. Brettle, 'Samuel Daniel and the Children of the Queen's Revels, 1604–5,' *Review of English Studies*, 1927, pp. 162–168. Another explanation of Daniel's retirement is that it was due to the row over *Eastward Ho*.

had been duly perused by the Master of the Revels. But although he added, inadvisedly, that part of it had also been read to Mountjoy, now Earl of Devonshire, he did not say that Mountjoy (who was sensitive about the Essex affair) had countenanced its performance — and, indeed, there would have been no performance 'had not his necessities overmaistred him.' * The good faith of these statements is not, I think, to be questioned, but the seriousness of the charges comes out when the resemblances between Essex and Philotas are perceived. The danger in which the poet had stood was a real one, and the manliness of his Apology (affixed to the printed play) is all the more to his credit. The last words are:

And for any resemblance, that thorough the ignorance of the History may be applied to the late Earle of *Essex*, it can hold in no proportion but only in his weaknesses, which I would wish all that loue his memory not to reuiue. And for mine owne part, hauing beene perticularly beholding to his bounty, I would to God his errors and disobedience to his Souereigne, might be so deepe buried vnderneath the earth, and in so low a tombe from his other parts, that hee might neuer be remembred among the examples of disloyalty in this Kingdome, or paraleld with Forreine Conspirators.

Daniel's feelings had been deeply wounded. In dedicating *Philotas* to Prince Henry, he writes of himself as '*the remnant of another time*,' one who has '*outliu'd the date/Of former grace, acceptance and delight.*'

* The quotations are from his letters to Mountjoy and Lord Cranborne, as printed in Sellers's 'Bibliography of the Works of Samuel Daniel 1585–1623' (*Oxford Bibliographical Society, Proceedings and Papers*, vol. II, part i, 1927). Mr. Brettle's documents show that Daniel had been driven to get advances on his annuity, and that these advances sometimes went 'to oth[ers] to whom the said Danyell did stande indebted.'

He even wishes that his verses had never come to light:

> So had I not beene tax'd for wishing well,
> Nor now mistaken by the censuring Stage,
> Nor, in my fame and reputation fell,
> Which I esteeme more then what all the age
> Or th'earth can giue. But yeeres hath done this wrong,
> To make me write too much, and liue too long.

'In his old Age,' Fuller says 'he turn'd *Husbandman*, and Rented a Farm in *Wiltshire*,' and this retirement seems to have begun soon after the *Philotas* incident. A letter of 1608, only lately brought to light, shows him concerned over hay which would not sell 'at any rate reasonable,' and counting up the pigeons he had been eating and owed for — 'so many pigions,' too! As for 'Kent & yᵗ pore side of yᵉ world,' it seemed now 'out of Christendome, or els I ame turnd renegado.' * Still, he must have continued to spend a good deal of time at court. As early as 1607 he signs himself 'one of the Groomes of the Queenes Maiesties priuie Chamber,' and his last work, *The Collection of the History of England*, was written for the most part 'vnder her Roofe, during his attendance vpon her Sacred Person.' It was for court performance, moreover, that he prepared two pastoral plays from Italian sources, *The Queen's Arcadia* (1605) and *Hymen's Triumph* (1614), and a second dull masque, *Tethys Festival* (1610). The pastorals are without Breton's details of actual English landscape or Fletcher's glamorous backgrounds for the *Faithful Shepherdess*. *The Queen's Arcadia* can claim to be the

* The letter — to one James Kirton — was first published by Sellers in *The Times Literary Supplement*, March 24, 1927.

first of its kind in English, and from *Hymen's Triumph* Charles Lamb culled one exquisite passage to immortalize among his *Specimens*. As for the *History*, though a first part came out as early as 1612, and though Daniel by no means began at the beginning — he repudiated Geoffrey of Monmouth's British kings, finding 'no authenticall warrant' for their existence — it remained, like *The Civil Wars*, unfinished, breaking off at '*the highest exaltation of this Kingdome*' under Edward the Third. Deeply-founded work, sagacious and independent, the *History* was once its author's most popular production. It is still an incomparable picture of his thought and opinions.

In 1615 Daniel seems to have been active in the establishing of a theatrical company at Bristol, but the patent he allowed to go to his brother John, a musician. There are references to the poet's failing health in 1618, and in October of the next year at Beckington (Somerset) he died. Simon Waterson, the publisher, was one of the overseers of his will. In it there is no reference to a wife; yet he had apparently had one (Fuller says her name was Justina), and the death of a 'M^rs. Daniell' is recorded in the Beckington Parish Register a few months before.* Anthony à Wood maintains that no less a personage than John Florio married Daniel's sister.†

Except for one agonizing moment, it must have been a tranquil life. 'As the *Tortoise* burieth himself all the Winter in the ground,' wrote Fuller, 'so M^r. *Daniel* would lye hid at his Garden-house in *Oldstreet*,

* For this find, I am again indebted to Mr. Sellers.

† His statement has been much questioned, but see Longworth Chambrun, *Giovanni Florio*, Paris, 1921, pp. 28 ff.

nigh *London*, for some Months together, (the more retiredly to enjoy the Company of the *Muses*,) and then would appear in publick, to converse with his Friends' — and no doubt call at the 'Signe of the Crowne' and see Master Waterson. It is almost a Victorian picture, and the recollection of Raleigh or Christopher Marlowe comes as a shock. So too, in characterizing Daniel's work, one instinctively begins with negatives. His vein was 'lofty,' indeed, but it was not 'insolent and passionate,' as well, like that of the giant race about him. The Elizabethan genius found its appropriate expression in the drama and the lyric. Daniel scarcely prevailed in either. If he began as a lyrical poet, it was with sonnets not songs, and the great work he left unfinished was in prose. His plays are closet-plays. He is without humor. In the *History*, after describing the institution of the Order of the Garter, he mentions the old story of the Countess of Salisbury's mishap, and says solemnly: 'But it were some derogation to that noble institution, to impute the originall thereof to an Act of Leuity, seeing with what a graue and religious Ceremony it is performed.' Then, with a touch of his best: 'Although, we see oftentimes, accidents of little consequence giue beginnings to things of great estimation, which time makes venerable.' *

His contemporaries pitched upon want of daring as his great fault — a want of daring which might lead to actual prosiness. He is 'well-languag'd Daniel,' whose 'rhymes were smooth'd with the file'; he 'might mount if he list,'

* v, 234.

Yet doth his trembling Muse but lowly flie,
As daring not too rashly mount on hight.

He should 'more sparingly make vse/Of others wit,'
and not be 'a Lucanist.' He was 'too much *Historian
in verse*' — 'his maner better fitted prose' — and
Ben called him 'a good honest man, but no poet.' *
As if echoing them, Daniel writes of 'irresolution and
a selfe distrust' as the 'most apparent faults' in his
nature: 'the least checke of reprehension, if it sauour
of reason, will as easily shake my resolution as any
mans liuing.' †

There is no note of distrust when he speaks of
poetry. He is sure of its validity, proud to be num-
bered among the poets; he knows that he will 'be
read, among the rest/So long as men speake english.' ‡ It is pointed out by Philocosmus that the
readers will be few. 'That few is all the world,' begins the reply:

> And for my part if onely one allow
>   The care my labouring spirits take in this,
>   He is to me a Theater large ynow,
>   And his applause only sufficient is:
>   All my respect is bent but to his brow,
>   That is my all, and all I am is his.
> And if some worthy spirits be pleased to,
>   It shall more comfort breed, but not more will;
>   But what if none; it cannot yet vndo
>   The loue I beare vnto this holy skill:
>   This is the thing that I was borne to do,
>   This is my Scene, this part must I fulfill. §

* Yet in later times it has been the poets who have read him. He was
a favorite with Coleridge and Wordsworth, and the subject of a too little
known essay by Thomas Gray.   † Page 130, below.
   ‡ *To the Reader*, ll. 59–60; compare *Cleopatra*, Dedication, l. 110.
   § Lines 567–578.

'*I had rather be Maister,*' he writes again, '*of a small peece handsomely contriued, then of vaste roomes ill proportioned and vnfurnished.*' * This does not sound like the authentic voice of one who erected such unwieldy structures as *The Civil Wars* and *The Collection of the History of England.* Yet he never forgot — as many of his fellows forgot — that as a poet he was called upon to write poetry. The 'building of his life' was a temple to Fame, and it behooved him to 'pull downe, raise, and reedifie,'

As if there were no saboath of the minde.†

Recognizing the impossibility of perfection, he yet labored to achieve perfection. Of the five longer pieces reprinted in this volume, *The Complaint of Rosamond* he revised at least five times, *Delia* four times, and years after writing *Musophilus* he all but ruined it. Through these revisions one sees an Elizabethan author in action. The aim of some of them was to improve the verbal melody of the lines. Others represent the conscientious excision of what he had come to regard as technical blemishes. Thus a 'kinde friend and countriman,' Master Hugh Samford, warned him, early in his career, againt the 'deformitie' of mingling feminine rhymes with masculine. Out they went — some harmless, some a bit Gilbertian — and he avoided their use thenceforward, and could congratulate himself that there were 'not aboue two couplettes in that kinde in all his Poem of the Ciuill warres.' ‡ That bane of actors, the Shakespearean dissyllabic *-ion*, had at one time appeared

* *History,* IV, 81.   † *To the Reader,* l. 15.
‡ *Defence of Ryme,* ll. 969 ff.

(xxxi)

frequently in his rhymes; but late in life he decided against it, purged *The Civil Wars* of it, and did what he could to purge the *Musophilus*.* Also, he went in for a general slaughter of expletives and interjections, especially of *O*'s. A desire for conciseness led him now and again to find one word for the two which had formerly satisfied him: Delia's 'faire bright starres' of eyes became 'radiant'; † and her poet's 'lamentable' songs had once been 'sad and mornefull.' ‡ He toiled at the achieving of clarity, sharpened his antitheses, toned down the exuberant hyperboles of a young fancy. An Elizabethan poet would, you might think, have remained confident that no reader could possibly mistake his metaphorical '*Cynthia*' of Sonnet XL for the name of a mistress (that a modern scholar succeeded in doing so, is beside the point). Daniel altered it, none the less, retrenching on his 'conceit' and referring to Delia — as Delia.

Kings cannot priuiledge a sinne forbade,§

he had made Rosamond say; then, as if it were a century later, he wrote in 'what God' for 'a sinne.' And indeed, if he was something of a 'belated humanist,' he was also, and most obviously in his revisions, something of a neo-classicist born before his time.

* *R*, 'the dog's letter,' was so fiercely spoken by the Elizabethans that it might, in verse, be made to produce an additional syllable where such was wanted. Daniel's ear, or perhaps his fingers, rejected the practice, and he rewrote a number of lines like
    And I, though borne in a colder clime,
(*Delia*, XXXV, l. 5) — in that instance changing 'in' to 'within.'
    † Page 180, ii, l. 2.
    ‡ III, l. 2.
    § Page 199, l. 70. *Delia*, XVI, l. 4, and XXIII, l. 9, are two more examples out of many.

As such, he became a stickler for accuracy. Delia's
'*Auon*' was not, he perceived, 'rich in fame': his in-
nate modesty, that 'selfe distrust' which he admitted
to be a fault, revolted at the pretence that it was.
'Poore in fame,' he calls it —

> No other prouder Brookes shall heare my wrong. *

His Philocosmus (in *Musophilus*) maintains that an
English poet may not hope to be read, even by Eng-
lishmen:

> How many thousands neuer heard the name
> Of *Sydney*, or of *Spencer*, or their bookes. . . . †

Daniel returned to the passage and changed the word
'heard' to 'weigh'! A greater poet was to stand con-
victed of the same error of literalization; but Milton,
after rewriting *Lycidas*, ll. 128–129,

> Besides what the grim Wolf with privy paw
> Daily devours apace, and *little* said,

came to his senses, and restored what he had first set
down — 'and *nothing* said.' ‡

In the eagerness and sincerity of his love of country
Daniel was at one with the men about him. To that
subject he never failed to respond with quickened
pulse and a renewed confidence in his own powers.
The pedestrianism of so much of his *Civil Wars* does

---

* *Delia*, XLVIII, ll. 11, 14.
† Lines 440–441.
‡ Several of the omissions in the 1607 volume are traceable, I believe,
to a timidity on the author's part, natural after *Philotas*. This will explain his deletion of the bawd's exegetical remarks on divine right (*Rosamond*, ll. 288–294), and some of the more violent utterances of Musophilus
(ll. 331–334, 677–790).

not extend to the pages in which he tells of Talbot and the Agincourt Harry. Margaret, a Frenchwoman, is blamed for the murder of good Duke Humphrey:

> Are these the deedes, high forraine wittes inuent?
> Is this that Wisedome whereof they so boast? . . .
>
> Let them haue fairer citties, goodlier soyles,
> And sweeter fieldes, for beautie to the eye,
> So long as they haue these vngodly wyles,
> Such detestable vile impietie:
> And let vs want their Vines, their Fruites the-whyles,
> So that wee want not fayth and honestie:
> We care not for those pleasures; so we may
> Haue better hearts, and stronger hands then they.*

And he calls upon Neptune to shut out such corruptions and 'keepe vs meere English.' What is more, this sentiment remained unsullied by Chauvinism. Daniel is cordial in his praises of the high qualities of former enemies — the courage of the Welsh, the 'Fortitude and Piety' of William Wallace. He is also quite aware that there are such things as unjust and unprofitable wars. Edward I is described as

A Prince of a generous spirit . . . watchfull and eager to enlarge his power: and was more for the greatnesse of *England*, then the quiet thereof. And this we may iustly say of him, that neuer King before, or since, shed so much Christian blood within this *Isle of Brittaine*, as this Christian Warrior did in his time, and was the cause of more in that following.†

And of Richard Coêur de Lion and his campaigns against the French Philip, it is recorded:

Foure yeares at least, held this miserable turmoyle betwixt these two kings, surprising, recouering, ruining and spoyling each

* *Civil Wars*, book v, stanzas 86, 87.
† *History*, v, 176.

others Estate, often deceiuing both the world, and themselues with shewe of couenants reconciliatory, which were euermore broken againe vppon all aduantages according to the Mystery of Warre and ambition.*

To his love of England he joined love of the past, sharing this with his master Sidney, with Spenser, and with not too many others among his contemporaries. Campion's slighting allusions to the Middle Ages offended him quite as much as did the vaunted infallibility of his Greeks and Romans. 'It is but the clowds gathered about our owne iudgement,' wrote Daniel, 'that makes vs thinke all other ages wrapt vp in mists, and the great distance betwixt vs, that causes vs to imagine men so farre off, to be so little in respect of our selues.' They were no 'deformed times' which fashioned 'the wonderfull Architecture of this state of *England*.' † Searching out the ruins of these elder years, he stands with something of awe before Stonehenge:

> Whereon when as the gazing passenger
>   Hath greedy lookt with admiration,
>   And faine would know his birth, and what he were,
>   How there erected, and how long agone:
>   Enquires and askes his fellow trauailer
>   What he hath heard and his opinion:
> And he knowes nothing. Then he turnes againe
>   And looks and sighs, and then admires afresh,
>   And in himselfe with sorrow doth complaine
>   The misery of darke forgetfulnesse.‡

* *Ibid.*, v, 23.
† *Defence of Ryme*, ll. 495–499, 584–585.
‡ *Musophilus*, ll. 343–352. In the *History*, he mentions some of the 'stately structures' erected in the twelfth century by Roger, Bishop of Sarum — 'of whose magnificence and spacious minde' they were 'memorialls left in notes of stone' (IV, 213); see also *Rosamond*, ll. 703–714.

Regretfully, he looks back to a golden time before the 'disordinate and lustfull' Henry, when the world was peaceful and devout, and men of learning lived in cloistered security. All illusion! He was even moved to write of how Nemesis gave 'gifts of griefe' to men: the printing-press, to disseminate controversy; gunpowder, to destroy 'th'antient forme and discipline of Warre.' * 'Some tax him to smack of the *Old Cask*,' wrote Fuller, 'as resenting of the *Romish Religion*'; then adds wisely, 'but they have a quicker Palate than I, who can make any such discovery.'

Yet Daniel's theme of themes has nothing to do with the past. A poet of the Renaissance, his imagination was fired by the Renaissance ideal of action — of 'high attempts,' 'motions of vnrest.' Taken up by him first in his sonnet days, it was developed in his great poem, *Musophilus*, and in *Ulisses and the Syren*, reappearing for the last time in *The Civil Wars*, just as he was turning from poetry. The introduction of this theme into the *Delia* (1594) could not be effected without dissonance. For twelve lines he triumphs:

> And yet I cannot reprehend the flight,
>> Or blame th'attempt presuming so to sore,
>> The mounting venter for a high delight,
>> Did make the honour of the fall the more.
> For who gets wealth that puts not from the shore?
>> Daunger hath honour, great designes their fame,
>> Glorie doth follow, courage goes before.
>> And though th'euent oft aunswers not the same,
> Suffise that high attempts haue neuer shame.
>> The Meane-obseruer, (whom base Safety keepes,)
>> Liues without honour, dies without a name,
>> And in eternall darknes euer sleepes.

* *Civil Wars*, book VI, stanzas 30 ff.

Then, when one looks for climax, for the pith and marrow of it all:

> And therefore DELIA, tis to me no blot,
> To haue attempted, though attain'd thee not.

At the end of *The Civil Wars*, Warwick is urged by his confessor to give over his turbulent desire, to rest, and live no longer 'perpetuall in disturbancy.' And the King-Maker replies:

> I knowe, that I am fixt vnto a Sphere
> That is ordayn'd to moue. It is the place
> My fate appoints me; and the region where
> I must, what-euer happens, there, imbrace.
> Disturbance, trauaile, labor, hope and feare,
> Are of that Clime, ingendred in that place;
> And action best, I see, becomes the Best:
> The Starres, that haue most glorie, haue no rest.*

But action alone is not enough: Philocosmus having but half the truth has none. And so in *Musophilus* Daniel sets out to reconcile the ideal of action with that of culture, 'of all *learning*':

> what good is like to this,
> To do worthy the writing, and to write
> Worthy the reading, and the worlds delight? †

As this theme possesses him, he fairly comes into his own. The spirit of the voyagers, of enduring youth, shines through the last verses of the poem. In them he prophesies: of the new world that is to continue the civilization of the old, of the great poet who is to express that civilization at its finest. It is, after all, when he is most an Elizabethan that Daniel comes nearest to being something more.

* Book VIII, stanza 104.   † Lines 198–200.

Poems

AND

A Defence of Ryme

To the Reader

To the Reader

BEhold once more with serious labor here
Haue I refurnisht out this little frame,
Repaird some parts defectiue here and there,
And passages new added to the same, (were
Some rooms inlargd, made some les thẽ they
Like to the curious builder who this yeare
Puls downe, and alters what he did the last
As if the thing in doing were more deere
Then being done, & nothing likes thats past   10
   For that we euer make the latter day
The scholler of the former, and we find
Something is still amisse that must delay
Our busines, and leaue worke for vs behinde.
As if there were no saboath of the minde.
And howsoeuer be it well or ill
What I haue done, it is mine owne I may
Do whatsoeuer therewithall I will.
   I may pull downe, raise, and reedifie
It is the building of my life the fee   20
Of Nature, all th'inheritance that I
Shal leaue to those which must come after me
And all the care I haue is but to see
These lodgings of m'affections neatly drest
Wherein so many noble friends there be
Whose memories with mine must therin rest
And glad I am that I haue liud to see
This edifice renewd, who doo but long
To liue t'amend. For man is a tree
That hath his fruite late ripe, and it is long   30
Before he come t'his taste, there doth belong

So much t'experience, and so infinite
The faces of things are, as hardly we
Discerne which lookes the likest vnto right.
    Besides these curious times stuf'd with the
Of cõpositions in this kind, do driue (store
Me to examine my defects the more,
And oft would make me not my self belieue
Did I not know the world wherein I liue,
Which neither is so wise, as that would seeme   40
Nor certaine iudgement of those things doth
That it disliks, nor that it doth esteeme. (giue
    I know no work from man yet euer came
But had his marke, and by some error shewd
That it was his, and yet what in the same
Was rare, an worthy, euermore allowd
Safe cõuoy for the rest: the good thats sow'd
Thogh rarely paies our cost, & who so looks
T'haue all thinges in perfection, & in frame
In mens inuentions, neuer must read books.   50
    And howsoeuer here detraction may
Disvalew this my labour, yet I know
There wilbe foũd therin, that which wil pay
The reckning for the errors which I owe
And likewise will sufficiently allow
T'an vndistasted iudgement fit delight
And let presumptuous selfe-opinion say
The worst it can, I know I shall haue right.
    I know I shalbe read, among the rest
So long as men speake english, and so long   60
As verse and vertue shalbe in request
Or grace to honest industry belong:
And England since I vse thy present tongue
Thy forme of speech thou must be my defẽce
If to new eares, it seemes not well exprest
For though I hold not accent I hold sence.

(4)

And since the measures of our tong we see
Confirmd by no edict of power doth rest
But onely vnderneath the regencie
Of vse and fashion, which may be the best   70
Is not for my poore forces to contest
But as the Peacock, seeing himselfe to weake
Confest the Eagle fairer farre to be
And yet not in his feathers but his beake.
Authoritie of powerfull censure may
Preiudicate the forme wherein we mould
This matter of our spirite, but if it pay (wold
The eare with substance, we haue what wee
For that is all which must our credit hold.
The rest (how euer gay, or seeming rich   80
It be in fashion, wise men will not wey)
The stamp will not allow it, but the touch.
    And would to God that nothing falty were
But only that poore accent in my verse
Or that I could all other recknings cleere
Wherwith my heart stands charg'd, or might
The errors of my iudgmẽt passed here (revers
Or els where, in my bookes, and vnrehearce
What I haue vainely said, or haue addrest
Vnto neglect mistaken in the rest.   90
    Which I do hope to liue yet to retract
And craue that England neuer wil take note
That it was mine. Ile disavow mine act,
And wish it may for euer be forgot,
I trust the world will not of me exact
Against my will, that hath all els I wrote,
I will aske nothing therein for my paine
But onely to haue in mine owne againe.

Delia

Delia.

Contayning certayne
Sonnets: vvith the
complaint of
Rosamond.

(.˙.)

 Aetas prima canat Veneres
postrema tumultus.

AT LONDON,
Printed by I. C. for Si-
mon Waterson, dwelling in
Paules Church-yard at
the signe of the Crowne.
1592.

TO THE RIGHT HO-
nourable the Ladie *Mary,*
Countesse of Pembroke.

RIght honorable, although I rather desired to keep in
the priuate passions of my youth, from the multi-
tude, as things vtterd to my selfe, and consecrated to
silence: yet seeing I was betraide by the indiscretion of a
greedie Printer, and had some of my secrets bewraide to
the world, vncorrected: doubting the like of the rest, I am
forced to publish that which I neuer ment. But this 10
wrong was not onely doone to mee, but to him whose vn-
matchable lines haue indured the like misfortune; Ignor-
ance sparing not to commit sacriledge vpon so holy
Reliques. Yet Astrophel, *flying with the wings of his*
own fame, a higher pitch then the gross-sighted can dis-
cerne, hath registred his owne name in the Annals of
eternitie, and cannot be disgraced, howsoeuer disguised.
And for my selfe, seeing I am thrust out into the worlde,
and that my vnboldned Muse, is forced to appeare so
rawly in publique; I desire onely to bee graced by the 20
countenance of your protection: whome the fortune of our
time hath made the happie and iudiciall Patronesse of
the Muses, (a glory hereditary to your house) to preserue
them from those hidious Beastes, Obliuion, and Bar-
barisme. Whereby you doe not onely possesse the honour
of the present, but also do bind posterity to an euer grate-
full memorie of your vertues, wherein you must suruiue
your selfe. And if my lines heereafter better laboured,
shall purchase grace in the world, they must remaine the
monuments of your honourable fauour, and recorde the 30
zealous duetie of mee, who am vowed to your honour in
all obseruancy for euer,

Samuel Danyell.

(9)

TO DELIA.

Sonnet I.

Vnto the boundles Ocean of thy beautie
Runs this poore riuer, charg'd with streames of zeale:
Returning thee the tribute of my dutie,
Which heere my loue, my youth, my playnts reueale.
    Heere I vnclaspe the booke of my charg'd soule,
Where I haue cast th'accounts of all my care:
Heere haue I summ'd my sighes, heere I enroule
Howe they were spent for thee; Looke what they are.
    Looke on the deere expences of my youth,
And see how iust I reckon with thyne eyes:
Examine well thy beautie with my trueth,
And crosse my cares ere greater summes arise. (slightly;
        Reade it sweet maide, though it be doone but
        Who can shewe all his loue, doth loue but lightly.

Sonnet II.

Goe wailing verse, the infants of my loue,
Minerua-like, brought foorth without a Mother:
Present the image of the cares I proue,
Witnes your Fathers griefe exceedes all other.
    Sigh out a story of her cruell deedes,
With interrupted accents of dispayre:
A Monument that whosoeuer reedes,
May iustly praise, and blame my loueles Faire.
    Say her disdaine hath dryed vp my blood,
And starued you, in succours still denying:
Presse to her eyes, importune me some good;
Waken her sleeping pittie with your crying.   (her;
        Knock at that hard hart, beg till you haue moou'd
        And tell th'vnkind, how deerely I haue lou'd her.

Sonnet III.

If so it hap this of-spring of my care,
These fatall Antheames, sad and mornefull Songes:
Come to their view, who like afflicted are;
Let them yet sigh their owne, and mone my wrongs.
    But vntouch'd harts, with vnaffected eye,
Approch not to behold so great distresse:
Cleer-sighted you, soone note what is awry,
Whilst blinded ones mine errours neuer gesse.
    You blinded soules whom youth and errours lead,
You outcast Eglets, dazled with your sunne:
Ah you, and none but you my sorrowes read,
You best can iudge the wrongs that she hath dunne.
      That she hath doone, the motiue of my paine;
      Who whilst I loue, doth kill me with disdaine.

Sonnet IIII.

These plaintiue verse, the Posts of my desire,
Which haste for succour to her slowe regarde:
Beare not report of any slender fire,
Forging a griefe to winne a fames rewarde.
    Nor are my passions limnd for outward hewe,
For that no collours can depaynt my sorrowes:
Delia her selfe, and all the world may viewe
Best in my face, how cares hath til'd deepe forrowes.
    No Bayes I seeke to deck my mourning brow,
O cleer-eyde Rector of the holie Hill:
My humble accents craue the Olyue bow,
Of her milde pittie and relenting will.
      These lines I vse, t'unburthen mine owne hart;
      My loue affects no fame, nor steemes of art.

Sonnet V.

Whilst youth and error led my wandring minde,
And set my thoughts in heedeles waies to range:
All vnawares a Goddesse chaste I finde,
Diana-like, to worke my suddaine change.
    For her no sooner had my view bewrayd,
But with disdaine to see me in that place:
With fairest hand, the sweet vnkindest maide,
Castes water-cold disdaine vpon my face.
    Which turn'd my sport into a Harts dispaire,
Which still is chac'd, whilst I haue any breath,
By mine owne thoughts: set on me by my faire,
My thoughts like houndes, pursue me to my death.
        Those that I fostred of mine owne accord,
        Are made by her to murther thus their Lord.

Sonnet VI.

Faire is my loue, and cruell as sh'is faire;
Her brow shades frownes, although her eyes are sunny;
Her Smiles are lightning, though her pride dispaire;
And her disdaines are gall; her fauours hunny.
    A modest maide, deckt with a blush of honour,
Whose feete doe treade greene pathes of youth and loue,
The wonder of all eyes that looke vppon her:
Sacred on earth, design'd a Saint aboue.
    Chastitie and Beautie, which were deadly foes,
Liue reconciled friends within her brow:
And had she pittie to conioine with those,
Then who had heard the plaints I vtter now.
        O had she not beene faire, and thus vnkinde,
        My Muse had slept, and none had knowne my
                                            (minde.

(13)

Sonnet VII.

O had she not beene faire and thus vnkinde,
Then had no finger pointed at my lightnes:
The world had neuer knowne what I doe finde,
And Clowdes obscure had shaded still her brightnes.

Then had no Censors eye these lines suruaide,
Nor grauer browes haue iudg'd my Muse so vaine;
No sunne my blush and errour had bewraide,
Nor yet the world had heard of such disdaine.

Then had I walkt with bold erected face,
No down-cast looke had signified my mis:
But my degraded hopes, with such disgrace
Did force me grone out griefes, and vtter this.

  For being full, should not I then haue spoken:
  My sence oppres'd, had fail'd; and hart had broken.

Sonnet VIII.

Thou poore hart sacrifiz'd vnto the fairest,
Hast sent the incens of thy sighes to heauen:
And still against her frownes fresh vowes repayrest,
And made thy passions with her beautie euen.

And you mine eyes the agents of my hart,
Told the dumbe message of my hidden griefe:
And oft with carefull turnes, with silent art,
Did treate the cruell Fayre to yeelde reliefe.

And you my verse, the Aduocates of loue,
Haue followed hard the processe of my case:
And vrg'd that title which dooth plainely proue,
My faith should win, if iustice might haue place.

  Yet though I see, that nought we doe can moue her,
  Tis not disdaine must make me leaue to loue her.

Sonnet IX.

If this be loue, to drawe a weary breath,
Painte on flowdes, till the shore, crye to th'ayre:
With downward lookes, still reading on the earth;
The sad memorials of my loues despaire.

If this be loue, to warre against my soule,
Lye downe to waile, rise vp to sigh and grieue me:
The neuer-resting stone of care to roule,
Still to complaine my greifes, and none releiue me.

If this be loue, to cloath me with darke thoughts,
Haunting vntroden pathes to waile apart;
My pleasures horror, Musique tragicke notes,
Teares in my eyes, and sorrowe at my hart.

    If this be loue, to liue a liuing death;
    O then loue I, and drawe this weary breath.

Sonnet X.

O then I loue, and drawe this weary breath,
For her the cruell faire, within whose brow
I written finde the sentence of my death,
In vnkinde letters; wrought she cares not how.

O thou that rul'st the confines of the night,
Laughter-louing Goddesse, worldly pleasures Queene,
Intenerat that hart that sets so light,
The truest loue that euer yet was seene.

And cause her leaue to triumph in this wise,
Vppon the prostrate spoyle of that poore harte:
That serues a trophey to her conquering eyes,
And must their glorie to the world imparte.   (me;

    Once let her know, sh'hath done enough to proue
    And let her pittie if she cannot loue me.

Sonnet XI.

Teares, vowes, and prayers win the hardest hart:
Teares, vowes, and prayers haue I spent in vaine;
Teares, cannot soften flint, nor vowes conuart,
Prayers preuaile not with a quaint disdaine.

I lose my teares, where I haue lost my loue,
I vowe my faith, where faith is not regarded;
I pray in vaine, a merciles to moue:
So rare a faith ought better be rewarded.

Yet though I cannot win her will with teares,
Though my soules Idoll scorneth all my vowes;
Though all my prayers be to so deafe eares:
No fauour though the cruell faire allowes.

Yet will I weepe, vowe, pray to cruell Shee;
Flint, Frost, Disdaine, weares, melts, and yeelds
(we see.

Sonnet XII.

My spotles loue hoouers with white wings,
About the temple of the proudest frame:
Where blaze those lights fayrest of earthly things,
Which cleere our clouded world with brightest flame.

M'ambitious thoughts confined in her face,
Affect no honour, but what she can giue mee:
My hopes doe rest in limits of her grace,
I weygh no comfort vnlesse she releeue mee.

For she that can my hart imparadize,
Holdes in her fairest hand what deerest is:
My fortunes wheele, the circle of her eyes,
Whose rowling grace deigne once a turne of blis.

All my liues sweete consists in her alone,
So much I loue the most vnlouing one.

Sonnet XIII.

Behold what happe *Pigmaleon* had to frame,
And carue his proper griefe vpon a stone:
My heauie fortune is much like the same,
I worke on Flint, and that's the cause I mone.
　　For haples loe euen with mine owne desires,
I figured on the table of my harte,
The fayrest forme, the worldes eye admires,
And so did perish by my proper arte.
　　And still I toile, to chaunge the marble brest
Of her, whose sweetest grace I doe adore:
Yet cannot finde her breathe vnto my rest,
Hard is her hart and woe is me therefore.
　　　　O happie he that ioy'd his stone and arte,
　　　　Vnhappy I to loue a stony harte.

Sonnet XIIII.

Those amber locks, are those same nets my deere,
Wherewith my libertie thou didst surprize:
Loue was the flame, that fired me so neere,
The darte transpearsing, were those Christall eyes.
　　Strong is the net, and feruent is the flame;
Deepe is the wounde, my sighes do well report:
Yet doe I loue, adore, and praise the same,
That holdes, that burnes, that wounds me in this sort.
　　And list not seeke to breake, to quench, to heale,
The bonde, the flame, the wound that festreth so;
By knife, by lyquor, or by salue to deale:
So much I please to perish in my wo.
　　　　Yet least long trauailes be aboue my strength,
　　　　Good *Delia* lose, quench, heale me now at length.

Sonnet XV.

If that a loyall hart and faith vnfained,
If a sweete languish with a chast desire:
If hunger-staruen thoughts so long retayned,
Fed but with smoake, and cherisht but with fire.

And if a brow with cares caracters painted,
Bewraies my loue, with broken words halfe spoken,
To her that sits in my thoughts Temple sainted,
And layes to view my Vultur-gnawne hart open.

If I haue doone due homage to her eyes,
And had my sighes styll tending on her name:
If on her loue my life and honour lyes;
And she th'vnkindest maide still scornes the same.

    Let this suffice, the world yet may see;
    The fault is hers, though mine the hurt must bee.

Sonnet XVI.

Happie in sleepe, waking content to languish,
Imbracing cloudes by night, in day time morne:
All things I loath saue her and mine owne anguish,
Pleas'd in my hurt, inur'd to liue forlorne.

Nought doe I craue, but loue, death, or my Lady,
Hoarce with crying mercy, mercy yet my merit;
So many vowes and prayers euer made I,
That now at length t'yeelde, meere pittie were it.

But still the *Hydra* of my cares renuing,
Reuiues new sorrowes of her fresh disdayning;
Still must I goe the Summer windes pursuing:
Finding no ende nor Period of my payning.

    Waile all my life, my griefes do touch so neerely,
    And thus I liue, because I loue her deerely.

Sonnet XVII.

Since the first looke that led me to this error,
To this thoughts-maze, to my confusion tending:
Still haue I liu'd in griefe, in hope, in terror,
The circle of my sorrowes neuer ending.

Yet cannot leaue her loue that holdes me hatefull,
Her eyes exact it, though her hart disdaines mee:
See what reward he hath that serues th'vngratefull,
So true and loyall loue no fauours gaines mee.

Still must I whet my younge desires abated,
Vppon the Flint of such a hart rebelling;
And all in vaine, her pride is so innated,
She yeeldes no place at all for pitties dwelling.

Oft haue I tolde her that my soule did loue her,
And that with teares, yet all this will not moue her.

Sonnet XVIII.

Restore thy tresses to the golden Ore,
Yeelde *Cithereas* sonne those Arkes of loue;
Bequeath the heauens the starres that I adore,
And to th'Orient do thy Pearles remoue.

Yeelde thy hands pride vnto th'yuory whight,
T'*Arabian* odors giue thy breathing sweete:
Restore thy blush vnto *Aurora* bright,
To *Thetis* giue the honour of thy feete.

Let *Venus* haue thy graces, her resign'd,
And thy sweete voyce giue backe vnto the Spheares:
But yet restore thy fearce and cruell minde,
To *Hyrcan* Tygers, and to ruthles Beares.

Yeelde to the Marble thy hard hart againe;
So shalt thou cease to plague, and I to paine.

Sonnet XIX.

If Beautie thus be clouded with a frowne,
That pittie shines no comfort to my blis:
And vapors of disdaine so ouergrowne,
That my liues light thus wholy darkned is.
    Why should I more molest the world with cryes?
The ayre with sighes, the earth belowe with teares?
Since I liue hatefull to those ruthlesse eyes,
Vexing with vntun'd moane, her daintie eares.
    If I haue lou'd her deerer then my breath,
My breath that calls the heauens to witnes it:
And still must holde her deere till after death.
And if that all this cannot moue a whit;
       Yet let her say that she hath doone me wrong,
       To vse me thus and knowe I lou'd so long.

Sonnet XX.

Come death the Anchor-holde of all my thoughtes,
My last Resort whereto my soule appealeth;
For all too long on earth my fancy dotes,
Whilst my best blood my younge desiers sealeth.
    That hart is now the prospectiue of horror,
That honored hath the cruelst faire that lyueth:
The cruelst faire, that sees I languish for her,
Yet neuer mercy to my merit giueth.
    This is her Lawrell and her triumphes prize,
To tread me downe with foote of her disgrace:
Whilst I did builde my fortune in her eyes,
And laide my liues rest on so faire a face;
       That rest I lost, my loue, my life and all,
       So high attempts to lowe disgraces fall.

Sonnet XXI.

These sorrowing sighes, the smoakes of mine annoy;
These teares, which heate of sacred flame distils;
Are these due tributes that my faith dooth pay
Vnto the tyrant; whose vnkindnes kils.
　I sacrifize my youth, and blooming yeares,
At her proud feete, and she respects not it:
My flowre vntimely's withred with my teares,
And winter woes, for spring of youth vnfit.
　She thinkes a looke may recompence my care,
And so with lookes prolongs my long-lookt ease:
As short that blisse, so is the comfort rare,
Yet must that blisse my hungry thoughts appease.
　　Thus she returnes my hopes so fruitlesse euer,
　　Once let her loue indeede, or eye me neuer.

Sonnet XXII.

False hope prolongs my euer certaine griefe;
Traytrous to me and faithfull to my loue:
A thousand times it promis'd me reliefe,
Yet neuer any true effect I proue.
　Oft when I finde in her no trueth at all,
I banish her, and blame her trechery:
Yet soone againe I must her backe recall,
As one that dyes without her company.
　Thus often as I chase my hope from mee,
Straight way she hastes her vnto *Delias* eyes:
Fed with some pleasing looke there shall she bee,
And so sent backe and thus my fortune lyes.
　　Lookes feede my Hope, Hope fosters me in vaine;
　　Hopes are vnsure, when certaine is my paine.

Sonnet XXIII.

Looke in my griefes, and blame me not to morne,
From care to care that leades a life so bad;
Th'Orphan of fortune, borne to be her scorne,
Whose clouded brow dooth make my daies so sad.
　　Long are their nights whose cares doe neuer sleepe
Loathsome their daies, whome no sunne euer ioyde:
Her fairest eyes doe penetrate so deepe,
That thus I liue booth day and night annoyde.
　　But since the sweetest roote doth yeeld thus much,
Her praise from my complaint I may not part:
I loue th'effect for that the cause is such,
Ile praise her face, and blame her flintie hart.
　　　　Whilst that wee make the world admire at vs,
　　　　Her for disdaine, and me for louing thus.

Sonnet XXIIII.

Oft and in vaine my rebel thoughts haue ventred,
To stop the passage of my vanquisht hart:
And shut those waies my friendly foe first entred,
Hoping thereby to free my better part.
　　And whilst I garde these windowes of this forte,
Where my harts theefe to vexe me made her choice:
And thether all my forces doe transporte,
An other passage opens at her voice.
　　Her voyce betraies me to her hand and eye:
My freedomes tyrants conquering all by arte:
But ah, what glorie can she get thereby,
With three such powers to plague one silly harte.
　　　　Yet my soules soueraigne, since I must resigne;
　　　　Reigne in my thoughts, my loue and life are thine.

Sonnet XXV.

Raigne in my thoughts faire hand, sweete eye, rare
Possesse me whole, my harts triumuirat: (voyce,
Yet heauie hart to make so hard a choise,
Of such as spoile thy poore afflicted state,
    For whilst they striue which shall be Lord of all,
All my poore life by them is troden downe:
They all erect their Trophies on my fall,
And yeelde me nought that giues them their renowne.
    When backe I looke, I sigh my freedome past,
And waile the state wherein I present stande:
And see my fortune euer like to last,
Finding me rain'd with such a heauie hande;
      What can I doo but yeeld, and yeeld I doo,
      And serue all three, and yet they spoile me too.

Sonnet XXVI.

Whilst by her eyes pursu'd, my poore hart flew it,
Into the sacred bosome of my deerest:
She there in that sweete sanctuary slew it,
Where it presum'd his safetie to be neerest.
    My priuiledge of faith could not protect it,
That was with blood and three yeeres witnes signed:
In all which time she neuer could suspect it,
For well she sawe my loue, and how I pined.
    And yet no comfort would her brow reueale mee,
No lightning looke, which falling hopes erecteth:
What bootes to lawes of succour to appeale mee?
Ladies and tyrants, neuer lawes respecteth.
      Then there I dye, where hop'd I to haue liuen;
      And by that hand, which better might haue giuen.

Sonnet XXVII.

The starre of my mishappe impos'd this payning,
To spend the Aprill of my yeers in wayling,
That neuer found my fortune but in wayning,
With still fresh cares my present woes assayling.
    Yet her I blame not, though she might haue blest
But my desires wings so high aspiring: (mee,
Now melted with the sunne that hath possest mee,
Downe doe I fall from off my high desiring;
    And in my fall doe cry for mercy speedy,
No pittying eye lookes backe vppon my mourning:
No helpe I finde when now most fauour neede I,
Th'Ocean of my teares must drowne me burning,
        And this my death shall christen her anew,
        And giue the cruell Faire her tytle dew.

Sonnet XXVIII.

Raysing my hopes on hills of high desire,
Thinking to skale the heauen of her hart:
My slender meanes presum'd too high a part;
Her thunder of disdaine forst me retire;
    And threw mee downe to paine in all this fire,
Where loe I languish in so heauie smart,
Because th'attempt was farre aboue my arte:
Her pride brook'd not poore soules shold come so nye
    Yet I protest my high aspyring will,   (her.
Was not to dispossesse her of her right:
Her soueraignty should haue remayned still,
I onely sought the blisse to haue her sight.
        Her sight contented thus to see me spill,
        Fram'd my desires fit for her eyes to kill.

Sonnet XXIX.

O why dooth *Delia* credite so her glasse,
Gazing her beautie deign'd her by the skyes:
And dooth not rather looke on him (alas)
Whose state best shewes the force of murthering eyes.

　The broken toppes of loftie trees declare,
The fury of a mercy-wanting storme:
And of what force your wounding graces are,
Vppon my selfe you best may finde the forme.

　Then leaue your glasse, and gaze your selfe on mee,
That Mirrour shewes what powre is in your face:
To viewe your forme too much, may daunger bee,
Narcissus chaung'd t'a flowre in such a case.

　　And you are chaung'd, but not t'a Hiacint;
　　I feare your eye hath turn'd your hart to flint.

Sonnet XXX.

I once may see when yeeres shall wrecke my wronge,
When golden haires shall chaunge to siluer wyer:
And those bright rayes, that kindle all this fyer
Shall faile in force, their working not so stronge.

　Then beautie, now the burthen of my song,
Whose glorious blaze the world dooth so admire;
Must yeelde vp all to tyrant Times desire:
Then fade those flowres which deckt her pride so long.

　When if she grieue to gaze her in her glas,
Which then presents her winter-withered hew;
Goe you my verse, goe tell her what she was;
For what she was she best shall finde in you.

　　Your firie heate lets not her glorie passe,
　　But Phenix-like shall make her liue anew.

Sonnet XXXI.

Looke *Delia* how wee steeme the half-blowne Rose,
The image of thy blush and Summers honor:
Whilst in her tender greene she doth inclose
That pure sweete beautie, Time bestowes vppon her.
  No sooner spreades her glorie in the ayre,
But straight her ful-blowne pride is in declyning;
She then is scorn'd that late adorn'd the fayre:
So clowdes thy beautie, after fayrest shining.
  No Aprill can reuiue thy withred flowers,
Whose blooming grace adornes thy glorie now:
Swift speedy Time, feathred with flying howers,
Dissolues the beautie of the fairest brow.
    O let not then such riches waste in vaine;
    But loue whilst that thou maist be lou'd againe.

Sonnet XXXII.

But loue whilst that thou maist be lou'd againe,
Now whilst thy May hath fill'd thy lappe with flowers;
Now whilst thy beautie beares without a staine;
Now vse thy Summer smiles ere winter lowres.
  And whilst thou spread'st vnto the rysing sunne,
The fairest flowre that euer sawe the light:
Now ioye thy time before thy sweete be dunne,
And *Delia*, thinke thy morning must haue night.
  And that thy brightnes sets at length to west:
When thou wilt close vp that which now thou showest:
And thinke the same becomes thy fading best,
Which then shall hide it most, and couer lowest.
    Men doe not weigh the stalke for that it was,
    When once they finde her flowre, her glory passe.

Sonnet XXXIII.

When men shall finde thy flowre, thy glory passe,
And thou with carefull brow sitting alone:
Receiued hast this message from thy glasse,
That tells thee trueth, and saies that all is gone.
　Fresh shalt thou see in mee the woundes thou madest,
Though spent thy flame, in mee the heate remayning:
I that haue lou'd thee thus before thou fadest,
My faith shall waxe, when thou art in thy wayning.
　The world shall finde this miracle in mee,
That fire can burne, when all the matter's spent:
Then what my faith hath beene thy selfe shalt see,
And that thou wast vnkinde thou maiest repent.
　Thou maist repent, that thou hast scorn'd my
(teares,
When Winter snowes vppon thy golden heares.

Sonnet XXXIIII.

When Winter snowes vpon thy golden heares,
And frost of age hath nipt thy flowers neere:
When darke shall seeme thy day that neuer cleares,
And all lyes withred that was held so deere.
　Then take this picture which I heere present thee,
Limned with a Pensill not all vnworthy:
Heere see the giftes that God and nature lent thee;
Heere read thy selfe, and what I suffred for thee.
　This may remaine thy lasting monument,
Which happily posteritie may cherish:
These collours with thy fading are not spent;
These may remaine, when thou and I shall perish.
　If they remaine, then thou shalt liue thereby;
They will remaine, and so thou canst not dye.

Sonnet XXXV.

Thou canst not dye whilst any zeale abounde
In feeling harts, that can conceiue these lines:
Though thou a *Laura* hast no *Petrarch* founde,
In base attire, yet cleerely Beautie shines.

And I, though borne in a colder clime,
Doe feele mine inward heate as great, I knowe it:
He neuer had more faith, although more rime,
I loue as well, though he could better shew it.

But I may ad one feather to thy fame,
To helpe her flight throughout the fairest Ile:
And if my penne could more enlarge thy name,
Then shouldst thou liue in an immortall stile.

But though that *Laura* better limned bee,
Suffice, thou shalt be lou'd as well as shee.

Sonnet XXXVI.

O be not grieu'd that these my papers should,
Bewray vnto the world howe faire thou art:
Or that my wits haue shew'd the best they could,
The chastest flame that euer warmed hart.

Thinke not sweete *Delia*, this shall be thy shame,
My Muse should sound thy praise with mournefull
How many liue, the glory of whose name,   (warble:
Shall rest in yce, when thine is grau'd in Marble.

Thou maist in after ages liue esteem'd,
Vnburied in these lines reseru'd in purenes;
These shall intombe those eyes, that haue redeem'd
Mee from the vulgar, thee from all obscurenes.

Although my carefull accents neuer mou'd thee;
Yet count it no disgrace that I haue lou'd thee.

Sonnet XXXVII.

Delia these eyes that so admireth thine,
Haue seene those walles the which ambition reared,
To checke the world, how they intombd haue lyen
Within themselues; and on them ploughes haue eared.

Yet for all that no barbarous hand attaynde,
The spoyle of fame deseru'd by vertuous men:
Whose glorious actions luckely had gainde,
Th'eternall Annals of a happie pen.

Why then though *Delia* fade let that not moue her,
Though time do spoyle her of the fairest vaile
That euer yet mortallitie did couer;
Which shall instarre the needle and the trayle.

That grace, that vertue, all that seru'd t'in-
Dooth her vnto eternitie assommon.   (woman;

Sonnet XXXVIII.

Faire and louely maide, looke from the shore,
See thy *Leander* striuing in these waues:
Poore soule fore-spent, whose force can doe no more,
Now send foorth hopes, for now calme pittie saues.

And wafte him to thee with those louely eyes,
A happy conuoy to a holy lande:
Now shew thy powre, and where thy vertue lyes,
To saue thine owne, stretch out the fayrest hand.

Stretch out the fairest hand a pledge of peace,
That hand that dartes so right, and neuer misses:
Ile not reuenge olde wrongs, my wrath shall cease;
For that which gaue me woundes, Ile giue it kisses.

Once let the Ocean of my cares finde shore,
That thou be pleas'd, and I may sigh no more.

Sonnet XXXIX.

Reade in my face, a volume of despayres,
The wayling Iliades of my tragicke wo;
Drawne with my bloud, and printed with my cares,
Wrought by her hand, that I haue honoured so.

Who whilst I burne, she singes at my soules wrack,
Looking a loft from Turret of her pride:
There my soules tyrant ioyes her, in the sack
Of her owne seate, whereof I made her guide.

There doe these smoakes that from affliction ryse,
Serue as an incense to a cruell Dame:
A Sacrifize thrice gratefull to her eyes,
Because their powre serue to exact the same.

    Thus ruines she, to satisfie her will;
    The Temple, where her name was honored still.

Sonnet XL.

My *Cynthia* hath the waters of mine eyes,
The ready handmaides on her grace attending:
That neuer fall to ebbe, nor euer dryes,
For to their flowe she neuer graunts an ending.

Th'Ocean neuer did attende more duely,
Vppon his Soueraignes course, the nights pale Queene:
Nor paide the impost of his waues more truely,
Then mine to her in truth haue euer beene.

Yet nought the rocke of that hard hart can moue,
Where beate these teares with zeale, and fury driueth:
And yet I rather languish in her loue
Then I would ioy the fayrest she that liueth.

    I doubt to finde such pleasure in my gayning,
    As now I taste in compas of complayning.

Sonnet XLI.

How long shall I in mine affliction morne,
A burthen to my selfe, distress'd in minde:
When shall my interdicted hopes returne,
From out despayre wherein they liue confin'd.
When shall her troubled browe charg'd with
                                    (disdaine,
Reueale the treasure which her smyles impart:
When shall my faith the happinesse attaine,
To breake the yce that hath congeald her hart.
Vnto her selfe, her selfe my loue dooth sommon,
If loue in her hath any powre to moue:
And let her tell me as she is a woman,
Whether my faith hath not deseru'd her loue.
    I knowe she cannot but must needes confesse it,
    Yet deignes not with one simple signe t'expresse it.

Sonnet XLII.

Beautie, sweet loue, is like the morning dewe,
Whose short refresh vpon the tender greene,
Cheeres for a time but tyll the Sunne doth shew,
And straight tis gone as it had neuer beene.
Soone doth it fade that makes the fairest florish,
Short is the glory of the blushing Rose,
The hew which thou so carefully doost nourish,
Yet which at length thou must be forc'd to lose.
When thou surcharg'd with burthen of thy yeeres,
Shalt bend thy wrinkles homeward to the earth:
When tyme hath made a pasport for thy feares,
Dated in age the Kalends of our death.
    But ah no more, thys hath beene often tolde,
    And women grieue to thinke they must be old.

Sonnet XLIII.

I must not grieue my Loue, whose eyes would reede,
Lines of delight, whereon her youth might smyle:
Flowers haue a tyme before they come to seede,
And she is young and now must sport the while.

Ah sport sweet Mayde in season of these yeeres,
And learne to gather flowers before they wither:
And where the sweetest blossoms first appeares,
Let loue and youth conduct thy pleasures thither.

Lighten forth smyles to cleere the clowded ayre,
And calme the tempest which my sighes doe rayse:
Pittie and smyles doe best become the fayre,
Pittie and smyles shall yeeld thee lasting prayse.

    I hope to say when all my griefes are gone,
    Happy the hart that sigh'd for such a one.

Sonnet XLIIII.

Drawne with th'attractiue vertue of her eyes,
My toucht hart turnes it to that happie cost:
My ioyfull North, where all my fortune lyes,
The leuell of my hopes desired most.

There where my *Delia* fayrer then the sunne,
Deckt with her youth whereon the world smyleth:
Ioyes in that honour which her beautie wonne,
Th'eternall volume which her fame compyleth.

Florish faire *Albion*, glory of the North,
Neptunes darling helde betweene his armes:
Deuided from the world as better worth,
Kept for himselfe, defended from all harmes.

    Still let disarmed peace decke her and thee;
    And Muse-foe *Mars*, abroade farre fostred bee.

Sonnet XLV.

Care-charmer sleepe, sonne of the Sable night,
Brother to death, in silent darknes borne:
Relieue my languish, and restore the light,
With darke forgetting of my cares returne.
  And let the day be time enough to morne,
The shipwrack of my ill-aduentred youth:
Let waking eyes suffice to wayle theyr scorne,
Without the torment of the nights vntruth.
  Cease dreames, th'ymagery of our day desires,
To modell foorth the passions of the morrow:
Neuer let rysing Sunne approue you lyers,
To adde more griefe to aggrauat my sorrow.
    Still let me sleepe, imbracing clowdes in vaine;
    And neuer wake, to feele the dayes disdayne.

Sonnet XLVI.

Let others sing of Knights and Palladines,
In aged accents, and vntimely words:
Paint shadowes in imaginary lines,
Which well the reach of their high wits records;
  But I must sing of thee and those faire eyes,
Autentique shall my verse in time to come,
When yet th'vnborne shall say, loe where she lyes,
Whose beautie made him speake that els was dombe.
  These are the Arkes the Tropheis I erect,
That fortifie thy name against old age,
And these thy sacred vertues must protect,
Against the Darke and times consuming rage.
    Though th'error of my youth they shall discouer,
    Suffice they shew I liu'd and was thy louer.

Sonnet XLVII.

Like as the Lute that ioyes or els dislikes,
As is his arte that playes vpon the same:
So sounds my Muse according as she strikes,
On my hart strings high tun'd vnto her fame.
    Her touch doth cause the warble of the sound,
Which heere I yeeld in lamentable wise,
A wailing deskant on the sweetest ground,
Whose due reports giue honor to her eyes.
    Els harsh my style, vntunable my Muse,
Hoarce sounds the voyce that prayseth not her name:
If any pleasing realish heere I vse,
Then iudge the world her beautie giues the same.
        O happie ground that makes the musique such,
        And blessed hand that giues so sweete a tuch.

Sonnet XLVIII.

None other fame myne vnambitious Muse,
Affected euer but t'eternize thee:
All other honours doe my hopes refuse,
Which meaner priz'd and momentarie bee.
    For God forbid I should my papers blot,
With mercynary lines, with seruile pen:
Praising vertues in them that haue them not,
Basely attending on the hopes of men.
    No no my verse respects nor Thames nor Theaters,
Nor seekes it to be knowne vnto the Great:
But *Auon* rich in fame, though poore in waters,
Shall haue my song, where *Delia* hath her seate.
        Auon shall be my Thames, and she my Song;
        Ile sound her name the Ryuer all along.

Sonnet XLIX.

Vnhappy pen and ill accepted papers,
That intimate in vaine my chaste desiers,
My chaste desiers, the euer burning tapers,
Inkindled by her eyes celestiall fiers.
  Celestiall fiers and vnrespecting powers,
That deigne not view the glory of your might,
In humble lines the worke of carefull howers,
The sacrifice I offer to her sight.
  But sith she scornes her owne, this rests for me,
Ile mone my selfe, and hide the wrong I haue:
And so content me that her frownes should be
To my' infant stile the cradle, and the graue.
    What though my selfe no honor get thereby,
    Each byrd sings t'herselfe, and so will I.

Sonnet L.

Loe heere the impost of a faith vnfaining,
That loue hath paide, and her disdaine extorted:
Beholde the message of my iust complayning,
That shewes the world how much my griefe imported.
  These tributary plaintes fraught with desire,
I sende those eyes the cabinets of loue;
The Paradice whereto my hopes aspire,
From out this hell, which mine afflictions proue.
  Wherein I thus doe liue cast downe from myrth,
Pensiue alone, none but despayre about mee;
My ioyes abortiue, perisht at their byrth,
My cares long liu'de, and will not dye without mee.
    This is my state, and *Delias* hart is such;
    I say no more, I feare I saide too much.

FINIS.

(35)

An Ode.

Nowe each creature ioyes the other,
  Passing happy daies and howers:
One byrd reports vnto another,
  In the fall of siluer showers,
Whilst the earth our common mother,
  Hath her bosome deckt with flowers.

Whilst the greatest torch of heauen,
  With bright rayes warmes *Floras* lappe:
Making nights and dayes both euen,
  Cheering plants with fresher sappe: 10
My field of flowers quite be-reauen,
  Wants refresh of better happe.

Eccho daughter of the ayre,
  Babbling gheste of Rocks and Hills,
Knowes the name of my fearce Fayre,
  And soundes the accents of my ills:
Each thing pitties my dispaire,
  Whilst that she her Louer kills.

Whilst that she O cruell Maide,
  Doth me, and my true loue dispise: 20
My liues florish is decayde
  That depended on her eyes:
But her will must be obaide,
  And well he'ends for loue who dies.

FINIS.

The Complaint of Rosamond

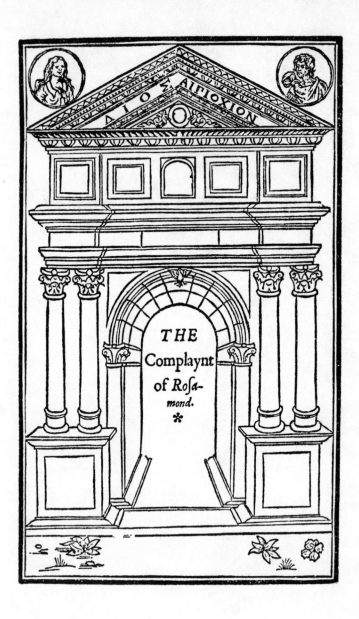

THE
Complaynt
of Roſa-
mond.
*

THE COMPLAINT OF
ROSAMOND.

OVT from the horror of infernall deepes,
  My poore afflicted ghost comes heere to plaine it:
Attended with my shame that neuer sleepes,
The spot wherewith my kinde, and youth did staine it:
My body found a graue where to containe it,
    A sheete could hide my face, but not my sin,
    For Fame finds neuer tombe t'inclose it in.

And which is worse, my soule is nowe denied,
Her transport to the sweet Elisean rest,
The ioyfull blisse for ghosts repurified,   10
The euer springing Gardens of the blest,
Caron denies me waftage with the rest.
    And sayes my soule can neuer passe that Riuer,
    Till Louers sighes on earth shall it deliuer.

So shall I neuer passe; for how should I
Procure this sacrifice amongst the liuing?
Time hath long since worne out the memorie,
Both of my life, and liues vniust depriuing:
Sorrow for me is dead for aye reuiuing.
    Rosamond hath little left her but her name,   20
    And that disgrac'd, for time hath wrong'd the
                                (same.
No Muse suggests the pittie of my case,
Each penne dooth ouerpasse my iust complaint,
Whilst others are preferd, though farre more base:
Shores wife is grac'd, and passes for a Saint;
Her Legend iustifies her foule attaint;
    Her well-told tale did such compassion finde,
    That she is pass'd, and I am left behinde.

Which seene with griefe, my myserable ghost,
(Whilome inuested in so faire a vaile,   30
Which whilst it liu'd, was honoured of the most,
And being dead, giues matter to bewaile)
Comes to sollicit thee, since others faile,
        To take this taske, and in thy wofull Song
        To forme my case, and register my wrong.

Although I knowe thy iust lamenting Muse,
Toylde in th'affliction of thine owne distresse,
In others cares hath little time to vse,
And therefore maist esteeme of mine the lesse:
Yet as thy hopes attend happie redresse,   40
        Thy ioyes depending on a womans grace,
        So moue thy minde a wofull womans case.

Delia may happe to deygne to read our story,
And offer vp her sigh among the rest,
Whose merit would suffice for both our glorie,
Whereby thou might'st be grac'd, and I be blest,
That indulgence would profit me the best;
        Such powre she hath by whom thy youth is lead,
        To ioy the liuing and to blesse the dead.

So I through beautie made the wofull'st wight,   50
By beautie might haue comfort after death:
That dying fayrest, by the fayrest might
Finde life aboue on earth, and rest beneath:
She that can blesse vs with one happy breath,
        Giue comfort to thy Muse to doe her best.
        That thereby thou maist ioy, and I might rest.

Thus saide: forthwith mou'd with a tender care
And pittie, which my selfe could neuer finde:
What she desir'd, my Muse deygn'd to declare,

And therefore will'd her boldly tell her minde:　60
And I more willing tooke this charge assignd,
　　Because her griefes were worthy to be knowne,
　　And telling hers, might hap forget mine owne.

Then write quoth shee the ruine of my youth,
Report the downe-fall of my slippry state:
Of all my life reueale the simple truth,
To teach to others, what I learnt too late:
Exemplifie my frailtie, tell howe Fate
　　Keepes in eternall darke our fortunes hidden,
　　And ere they come, to know them tis forbidden.　70

For whilst the sunn-shine of my fortune lasted,
I ioy'd the happiest warmth, the sweetest heat
That euer yet imperious beautie tasted,
I had what glory euer flesh could get:
But this faire morning had a shamefull set;
　　Disgrace darkt honor, sinne did clowde my brow,
　　As note the sequel, and Ile tell thee how.

The blood I staind was good and of the best,
My birth had honor, and my beautie fame:
Nature and Fortune ioyn'd to make me blest,　80
Had I had grace t'haue knowne to vse the same:
My education shew'd from whence I came,
　　And all concur'd to make me happy furst,
　　That so great hap might make me more accurst.

Happie liu'd I whilst Parents eye did guide,
The indiscretion of my feeble wayes:
And Country home kept me from being eyde,
Where best vnknowne I spent my sweetest dayes;
Till that my frindes mine honour sought to rayse,
　　To higher place, which greater credite yeeldes,　90
　　Deeming such beauty was vnfit for feeldes.

From Country then to Court I was preferr'd,
From calme to stormes, from shore into the deepes:
There where I perish'd, where my youth first err'd;
There where I lost the Flowre which honour keepes;
There where the worser thriues, the better weepes;
Ah me poore wench, on this vnhappy shelfe
I grounded me, and cast away my selfe.

For thither com'd, when yeeres had arm'd my youth
With rarest proofe of beautie euer seene: 100
When my reuiuing eye had learnt the truth,
That it had powre to make the winter greene,
And flowre affections whereas none had beene:
Soone could I teach my browe to tyrannize,
And make the world do homage to mine eyes.

For age I saw, though yeeres with cold conceit,
Congeald theyr thoughts against a warme desire:
Yet sigh their want, and looke at such a baite,
I saw how youth was waxe before the fire:
I saw by stealth, I fram'd my looke a lire,   110
Yet well perceiu'd how Fortune made me then,
The enuy of my sexe, and wonder vnto men.

Looke how a Comet at the first appearing,
Drawes all mens eyes with wonder to behold it:
Or as the saddest tale at suddaine hearing,
Makes silent listning vnto him that told it:
So did my speech when rubies did vnfold it;
So did the blasing of my blush appeere,
T'amaze the world, that holds such sights so deere.

Ah beauty Syren, fayre enchaunting good,   120
Sweet silent rethorique of perswading eyes:
Dombe eloquence, whose powre doth moue the blood,

More then the words, or wisedome of the wise:
Still harmonie, whose diapason lyes
    Within a brow, the key which passions moue,
    To rauish sence, and play a world in loue.

What might I then not doe whose powre was such?
What cannot women doe that know theyr powre?
What women knowes it not I feare too much,
How blisse or bale lyes in theyr laugh or lowre?   130
Whilst they enioy their happy blooming flowre,
    Whilst nature decks her with her proper fayre
    Which cheeres the worlde, ioyes each sight,
                        (sweetens th'ayre.

Such one was I, my beautie was mine owne,
No borrowed blush which banck-rot beauties seeke:
The new-found shame, a sinne to vs vnknowne,
Th'adulterate beauty of a falsed cheeke:
Vild staine to honor and to women eeke,
    Seeing that time our fading must detect,
    Thus with defect to couer our defect.   140

Impiety of times, chastities abator,
Falshod, wherein thy selfe, thy selfe deniest:
Treason, to counterfeit the seale of nature,
The stampe of heauen, impressed by the hiest.
Disgrace vnto the world, to whom thou lyest,
    Idol vnto thy selfe, shame to the wise,
    And all that honors thee idolatrise.

Farre was that sinne from vs whose age was pure,
When simple beautie was accounted best,
The time when women had no other lure   150
But modestie, pure cheekes, a vertuous brest:

This was the pompe wherewith my youth was blest;
These were the weapons which mine honour wunne
In all the conflicts that mine eyes begunne.

Which were not small, I wrought on no meane obiect;
A Crowne was at my feete, Scepters obaide mee:
Whom Fortune made my King, Loue made my Subiect,
Who did commaund the Land, most humbly praid mee:
Henry the second, that so highly weigh'd mee, 159
Founde well by proofe the priuiledge of Beautie,
That it hath powre to counter-maund all duetie.

For after all his victories in *Fraunce*,
Tryumphing in the honour of his deedes:
Vnmatch'd by sword, was vanquisht by a glaunce,
And hotter warres within his bosome breedes:
Warres whom whole Legions of desires feedes,
Against all which my chastity opposes,
The fielde of honour, vertue neuer loses.

No armour might bee founde that coulde defend,
Transpearcing rayes of Christall-pointed eyes: 170
No Stratagem, no reason could amend,
No not his age; yet olde men should be wise:
But shewes deceiue, outward appearance lyes;
Let none for seeming so, thinke Saints of others,
For all are men, and all haue suckt their Mothers.

Who would haue thought, a Monarch would haue euer
Obayed his handmaide, of so meane a state;
Vultur ambition feeding on his lyuer,
Age hauing worne his pleasures out of date:
But happe comes neuer or it comes too late, 180
For such a daintie which his youth found not,
Vnto his feeble age did chaunce allot.

Ah Fortune neuer absolutely good,
For that some crosse still counterchecks our luck:
As heere beholde th'incompatible blood,
Of age and youth was that whereon we stuck:
Whose loathing, we from natures brests do suck,
    As opposit to what our blood requires;
    For equall age doth equall like desires.

But mightie men in highest honor sitting,   190
Nought but applause and pleasure can behold:
Sooth'd in their liking, carelesse what is fitting,
May not be suffred once to thinke the'are old:
Not trusting what they see, but what is told.
    Miserable fortune to forget so farre,
    The state of flesh, and what our frailties are.

Yet must I needes excuse so great defect,
For drinking of the _Lethe_ of myne eyes:
H'is forc'd forget himselfe, and all respect
Of maiestie whereon his state relyes: 200
And now of loues, and pleasures must deuise.
    For thus reuiu'd againe, he serues and su'th,
    And seekes all meanes to vndermine my youth.

Which neuer by assault he could recouer,
So well incamp'd in strength of chaste desires:
My cleane-arm'd thoughts repell'd an vnchast louer,
The Crowne that could commaund what it requires,
I lesser priz'd then chastities attires,
    Th'vnstained vaile, which innocents adornes,
    Th'vngathred Rose, defended with the thornes. 210

And safe mine honor stoode till that in truth,
One of my Sexe, of place, and nature bad:
Was set in ambush to intrap my youth,

One in the habit of like frailtie clad,
One who the liu'ry of like weakenes had.
    A seeming Matrone, yet a sinfull monster,
    As by her words the chaster sort may conster.

Shee set vpon me with the smoothest speech,
That Court and age could cunningly deuise:
The one autentique made her fit to teach,   220
The other learnt her how to subtelise:
Both were enough to circumuent the wise.
    A document that well may teach the sage,
    That there's no trust in youth, nor hope in age.

Daughter (saith she) behold thy happy chaunce,
That hast the lot cast downe into thy lap,
Whereby thou maist thy honor great aduaunce,
Whilst thou (vnhappy) wilt not see thy hap:
Such fond respect thy youth doth so inwrap,   229
    T'oppose thy selfe against thine owne good fortune,
    That points thee out, and seemes thee to
                         (importune.

Doost thou not see how that thy King thy *Ioue*,
Lightens foorth glory on thy darke estate:
And showres downe golde and treasure from aboue,
Whilst thou doost shutte thy lappe against thy fate:
Fye fondling fye, thou wilt repent too late
    The error of thy youth; that canst not see
    What is the fortune that dooth followe thee.

Thou must not thinke thy flowre can alwayes florish,
And that thy beautie will be still admired: 240
But that those rayes which all these flames doe nourish,
Canceld with Time, will haue their date expyred,
And men will scorne what now is so desired:

Our frailtyes doome is written in the flowers,
Which florish now and fade ere many howers.

Reade in my face the ruines of my youth,
The wracke of yeeres vpon my aged brow:
I haue beene faire, I must confesse the trueth,
And stoode vppon as nice respects as thow;
I lost my time, and I repent it now;   250
     But were I to beginne my youth againe,
     I would redeeme the time I spent in vayne.

But thou hast yeeres and priuiledge to vse them,
Thy priuiledge doth beare beauties great seale:
Besides, the law of nature doth excuse them,
To whom thy youth may haue a iust appeale:
Esteeme not fame more then thou doost thy weale,
     Fame, wherof the world seemes to make such
     Is but an Eccho, and an idle voyce.   (choyce:

Then why should thys respect of honor bound vs,   260
In th'imaginary lists of reputation?
Titles which cold seueritie hath found vs,
Breath of the vulgar, foe to recreation:
Melancholies opinion, customs relation;   (fayre,
     Pleasures plague, beauties scourge, hell to the
     To leaue the sweete for Castles in the ayre.

Pleasure is felt, opinion but conceau'd,
Honor, a thing without vs, not our owne:
Whereof we see how many are bereau'd,
Which should haue rep'd the glory they had sowne,   270
And many haue it, yet vnworthy knowne.
     So breathes his blasts this many-headed beast,
     Whereof the wisest haue esteemed least.

The subtile Citty-women better learned,
Esteeme them chast ynough that best seeme so:
Who though they sport, it shall not be discerned,
Their face bewraies not what their bodies doe;
Tis warie walking that doth safliest goe.
 With shew of vertue, as the cunning knowes,
  Babes are beguild with sweetes, and men with
              (showes. 280

Then vse thy tallent, youth shall be thy warrant,
And let not honor from thy sports detract:
Thou must not fondly thinke thy selfe transparent,
That those who see thy face can iudge the fact;
Let her haue shame that cannot closely act.
 And seeme the chast, which is the cheefest arte,
  For what we seeme each sees, none knowes our
              (harte.

The mightie who can with such sinnes dispence,
In steed of shame doe honors great bestow:
A worthie author doth redeeme th'offence,   290
And makes the scarelet sinne as white as snow.
The Maiestie that doth descend so low,
 Is not defilde, but pure remaines therein:
  And being sacred, sanctifies the sin.

What, doost thou stand on thys, that he is olde,
Thy beauty hath the more to worke vppon:
Thy pleasures want shal be supply'd with gold,
Cold age dotes most when the heate of youth is gone:
Enticing words preuaile with such a one,   299
 Alluring shewes most deepe impression strikes,
  For age is prone to credite what it likes.

Heere interupt she leaues me in a doubt,
When loe began the combat in my blood:

Seeing my youth inuirond round about,
The ground vncertaine where my reasons stood;
Small my defence to make my party good,
     Against such powers which were so surely layde,
     To ouerthrow a poore vnskilful mayde.

Treason was in my bones my selfe conspyring,
To sell my selfe to lust, my soule to sinne: 310
Pure-blushing shame was euen in retiring,
Leauing the sacred hold it glory'd in.
Honor lay prostrate for my flesh to win,
     When cleaner thoughts my weakenes can vpbray
     Against my selfe, and shame did force me say.

Ah *Rosamond*, what doth thy flesh prepare,
Destruction to thy dayes, death to thy fame:
Wilt thou betray that honor held with care,
T''intombe with blacke reproch a spotted name,
Leauing thy blush the collours of thy shame.   320
     Opening thy feete to sinne, thy soule to lust,
     Gracelesse to lay thy glorie in the dust.

Nay first let th'earth gape wide to swallow thee,
And shut thee vp in bosome with her dead:
Ere Serpent tempt thee taste forbidden tree,
Or feele the warmth of an vnlawfull bed:
Suffring thy selfe by lust to be misled;
     So to disgrace thy selfe and grieue thine heires,
     That *Cliffords* race should scorne thee one of
                              (theyrs.

Neuer wish longer to inioy the ayre,   330
Then that thou breath'st the breath of chastitie:
Longer then thou preseru'st thy soule as faire
As is thy face, free from impuritie:
Thy face that makes th'admired in euery eye:

(49)

Where natures care such rarities inroule,
Which vs'd amisse, may serue to damne thy soule.

But what? he is my King and may constraine me,
Whether I yeelde or not I liue defamed:
The world will thinke authority did gaine me,
I shal be iudg'd hys loue, and so be shamed: 340
We see the fayre condemn'd, that neuer gamed.
     And if I yeeld, tis honorable shame,
     If not, I liue disgrac'd, yet thought the same.

What way is left thee then vnhappy mayde,
Whereby thy spotlesse foote may wander out
Thys dreadfull danger, which thou seest is layd,
Wherein thy shame doth compasse thee about?
Thy simple yeeres cannot resolue this doubt.
     Thy youth can neuer guide thy foote so euen,
     But in despight some scandall will be giuen.   350

Thus stood I ballanc'd equallie precize,
Till my fraile flesh did weigh me downe to sinne:
Till world and pleasure made me partialize,
And glittering pompe my vanitie did winne;
When to excuse my fault my lusts beginne,
     And impious thoughts alledg'd this wanton clause,
     That though I sinn'd, my sinne had honest cause.

So well the golden balles cast downe before me,
Could entertaine my course, hinder my way:
Whereat my rechlesse youth stooping to store me,   360
Lost me the gole, the glory, and the day.
Pleasure had set my wel-skoold thoughts to play,
     And bade me vse the vertue of mine eyes,
     For sweetly it fits the fayre to wantonise.

Thus wrought to sinne, soone was I traind from Court,
To a solitarie Grange there to attend
The time the King should thether make resort,
Where he loues long-desired work should end.
Thether he daily messages doth send,
      With costly iewels orators of loue: 370
      Which (ah too well men know) doe women moue.

The day before the night of my defeature,
He greets me with a Casket richly wrought:
So rare, that arte did seeme to striue with nature,
T'expresse the cunning work-mans curious thought;
The mistery whereof I prying sought.
      And found engrauen on the lidde aboue,
      Amymone how she with *Neptune* stroue.

Amymone old *Danaus* fayrest daughter,
As she was fetching water all alone   380
At *Lerna:* whereas *Neptune* came and caught her,
From whom she striu'd and strugled to be gone,
Beating the ayre with cryes and pittious mone.
      But all in vaine, with him sh'is forc'd to goe:
      Tis shame that men should vse poore maydens so.

There might I see described how she lay,
At those proude feete, not satisfied with prayer:
Wailing her heauie hap, cursing the day,
In act so pittious to expresse dispaire: 389
And by how much more greeu'd, so much more fayre;
      Her teares vpon her cheekes poore carefull gerle,
      Did seeme against the sunne cristall and perle.

Whose pure cleere streames, which loe so faire
Wrought hotter flames, O myracle of loue, (appeares,
That kindles fire in water, heate in teares,

And makes neglected beautie mightier proue:
Teaching afflicted eyes affects to moue;
  To shew that nothing ill becomes the fayre,
  But crueltie, that yeeldes vnto no prayer.

This hauing viewd and therewith something moued,
Figured I found within the other squares: 401
Transformed *Io, Ioues* deerely loued,
In her affliction how she strangely fares,
Strangelie distress'd, (O beautie borne to cares)
  Turn'd to a Heiffer, kept with iealous eyes,
  Alwaies in danger of her hatefull spyes.

These presidents presented to my view,
Wherein the presage of my fall was showne:
Might haue fore-warn'd me well what would ensue,
And others harmes haue made me shunne mine owne;
But fate is not preuented though fore-knowne.   411
  For that must hap decreed by heauenly powers,
  Who worke our fall, yet make the fault still ours.

Witnes the world, wherein is nothing rifer,
Then miseries vnkend before they come:
Who can the characters of chaunce discipher,
Written in clowdes of our concealed dome?
Which though perhaps haue beene reueald to some,
  Yet that so doubtfull as successe did proue them,
  That men must know they haue the heauens
            (aboue thẽ. 420

I sawe the sinne wherein my foote was entring,
I sawe how that dishonour did attend it,
I sawe the shame whereon my flesh was ventring,
Yet had I not the powre for to defende it;

(52)

So weake is sence when error hath condemn'd it:
    We see what's good, and thereto we consent vs;
    But yet we choose the worst, and soone repent vs.

And now I come to tell the worst of ilnes,
Now drawes the date of mine affliction neere:
Now when the darke had wrapt vp all in stilnes,   430
And dreadfull blacke, had dispossess'd the cleere:
Com'd was the night, mother of sleepe and feare,
    Who with her sable mantle friendly couers,
    The sweet-stolne sports, of ioyfull meeting Louers.

When loe I ioyde my Louer not my Loue,
And felt the hand of lust most vndesired:
Enforc'd th'vnprooued bitter sweete to proue,
Which yeeldes no mutuall pleasure when tis hired.
Loue's not constrain'd, nor yet of due required,
    Iudge they who are vnfortunately wed,   440
    What tis to come vnto a loathed bed.

But soone his age receiu'd his short contenting,
And sleepe seald vp his languishing desires:
When he turnes to his rest, I to repenting,
Into my selfe my waking thought retires:
My nakednes had prou'd my sences liers.
    Now opned were mine eyes to looke therein,
    For first we taste the fruite, then see our sin.

Now did I find my selfe vnparadis'd,
From those pure fieldes of my so cleane beginning: 450
Now I perceiu'd how ill I was aduis'd,
My flesh gan loathe the new-felt touch of sinning:
Shame leaues vs by degrees, not at first winning.
    For nature checks a new offence with lothing:
    But vse of sinne doth make it seeme as nothing.

And vse of sinne did worke in me a boldnes,
And loue in him, incorporates such zeale:
That iealosie increas'd with ages coldnes,
Fearing to loose the ioy of all his weale.
Or doubting time his stealth might els reueale,   460
    H'is driuen to deuise some subtile way,
    How he might safeliest keepe so rich a pray.

A stately Pallace he foorthwith did buylde,
Whose intricate innumerable wayes,
With such confused errors so beguil'd
Th'vnguided entrers with vncertaine strayes,
And doubtfull turnings kept them in delayes,
    With bootlesse labor leading them about,
    Able to finde no way, nor in, nor out.

Within the closed bosome of which frame,   470
That seru'd a Center to that goodly round:
Were lodgings, with a garden to the same,
With sweetest flowers that eu'r adorn'd the ground.
And all the pleasures that delight hath found,
    To entertaine the sence of wanton eyes,
    Fuell of loue, from whence lusts flames arise.

Heere I inclos'd from all the world a sunder,
The Minotaure of shame kept for disgrace:
The monster of fortune, and the worlds wonder,
Liu'd cloystred in so desolate a case: 480
None but the King might come into the place.
    With certaine maides that did attend my neede,
    And he himselfe came guided by a threed.

O Iealousie, daughter of enuy' and loue
Most wayward issue of a gentle Syer;
Fostred with feares, thy Fathers ioyes t'improue,

(54)

Myrth-marring Monster, borne a subtile lyer;
Hatefull vnto thy selfe, flying thine owne desier:
    Feeding vpon suspect that dooth renue thee,
    Happie were Louers if they neuer knewe thee. 490

Thou hast a thousand gates thou enterest by,
Conducting trembling passions to our hart:
Hundred eyed *Argos*, euer waking Spye,
Pale hagge, infernall fury, pleasures smart,
Enuious Obseruer, prying in euery part;
    Suspicious, fearefull, gazing still about thee,
    O would to God that loue could be without thee.

Thou didst depriue (through false suggesting feare)
Him of content, and me of libertie:
The onely good that women holde so deare,   500
And turnst my freedome to captiuitie,
First made a Prisoner, ere an enemy:
    Enioynd the raunsome of my bodies shame,
    Which though I paide could not redeeme the same.

What greater torment euer could haue beene,
Then to inforce the fayre to liue retired?
For what is Beautie if it be not seene,
Or what is't to be seene vnlesse admired?
And though admyred, vnlesse in loue desired?
    Neuer were cheekes of Roses, locks of Amber, 510
    Ordayn'd to liue imprisond in a Chamber.

Nature created Beautie for the view,
Like as the fire for heate, the Sunne for light:
The Faire doe holde this priuiledge as due,
By auncient Charter, to liue most in sight,
And she that is debarr'd it, hath not right.
    In vaine our friends in this vse their dehorting,
    For Beautie will be where is most resorting.

Witnes the fayrest streetes that Thames doth visit,
The wondrous concourse of the glittering Faire: 520
For what rare women deckt with Beautie is it,
That thither couets not to make repaire.
The solitary Country may not stay her,
      Heere is the center of all beauties best,
      Excepting *Delia*, left to adorne the West.

Heere doth the curious with iudiciall eyes,
Contemplate beauty gloriously attired:
And heerein all our cheefest glory lyes,
To liue where we are prais'd and most desired.
O how we ioy to see our selues admired,   530
      Whilst niggardly our fauours we discouer,
      We loue to be belou'd, yet scorne the Louer.

Yet would to God my foote had neuer moued
From Countrey safety, from the fields of rest:
To know the danger to be highly loued,
And lyue in pompe to braue among the best,
Happy for me, better had I beene blest;
      If I vnluckely had neuer strayde:
      But liu'd at home a happy Country mayde.

Whose vnaffected innocencie thinks   540
No guilefull fraude, as doth the Courtly liuer:
She's deckt with trueth, the Riuer where she drinks
Doth serue her for her glasse, her counsell giuer:
She loues sincerely, and is loued euer.
      Her dayes are peace, and so she ends her breath,
      True life that knowes not what's to die till death.

So should I neuer haue beene registred,
In the blacke booke of the vnfortunate:
Nor had my name enrold with Maydes misled,

Which bought theyr pleasures at so hie a rate.　550
Nor had I taught through my vnhappy fate,
　　This lesson which my selfe learnt with expence,
　　How most it hurts that most delights the sence.

Shame followes sinne, disgrace is duly giuen,
Impietie will out, neuer so closely doone:
No walles can hide vs from the eyes of heauen,
For shame must end what wickednesse begun:
Forth breakes reproch when we least thinke thereon.
　　And thys is euer propper vnto Courts:
　　That nothing can be doone but Fame reports.　560

Fame doth explore what lyes most secrete hidden,
Entring the closet of the Pallace dweller:
Abroade reuealing what is most forbidden,
Of trueth and falshood both an equall teller:
Tis not a guarde can serue for to expell her,
　　The sword of iustice cannot cutte her wings,
　　Nor stop her mouth from vtt'ring secrete things.

And this our stealth she could not long conceale,
From her whom such a forfeit most concerned:
The wronged Queene, who could so closely deale:　570
That she the whole of all our practise learned,
And watcht a time when least it was discerned,
　　In absence of the King, to wreake her wrong,
　　With such reuenge as she desired long.

The Laberinth she entred by that threed
That seru'd a conduct to my absent Lord:
Left there by chaunce, reseru'd for such a deede,
Where she surpriz'd me whom she so abhord.
Enrag'd with madnes, scarce she speakes a word,
　　But flyes with eger fury to my face,　580
　　Offring me most vnwomanly disgrace.

Looke how a Tygresse that hath lost her whelpe,
Runs fearcely raging through the woods astray:
And seeing her selfe depriu'd of hope or helpe,
Furiously assaults what's in her way,
To satisfie her wrath, not for a pray:
    So fell she on me in outragious wise,
    As could Disdaine and Iealousie deuise.

And after all her vile reproches vsed,
She forc'd me take the poyson she had brought: 590
To end the lyfe that had her so abused,
And free her feares, and ease her iealous thought.
No crueltie her wrath would leaue vnwrought,
    No spightfull act that to reuenge is common:
    For no beast fearcer then a iealous woman.

Those handes that beauties ministers had bin,
Must now gyue death, that me adorn'd of late:
That mouth that newly gaue consent to sin,
Must now receiue destruction in there-at.
That body which my lusts did violate,   600
    Must sacrifice it selfe t'appease the wrong,
    So short is pleasure, glory lasts not long.

The poyson soone disperc'd through all my vaines,
Had dispossess'd my liuing sences quite:
When naught respecting death, the last of paines,
Plac'd his pale collours, th'ensigne of his might,
Vpon hys new-got spoyle before his right;
    Thence chac'd my soule, setting my day ere noone,
    When I least thought my ioyes could end so soone.

And as conuaid t'vntimely funerals,   610
My scarce colde corse not suffred longer stay:
Behold the King (by chance) returning, falls

T'incounter with the same vpon the way,
As he repaird to see his deerest ioy.
    Not thinking such a meeting could haue beene,
    To see his loue, and seeing beene vnseene.

Iudge those whom chaunce depriues of sweetest
What tis to lose a thing we hold so deare: (treasure,
The best delight, wherein our soule takes pleasure,
The sweet of life, that penetrates so neare.   620
What passions feeles that hart, inforc'd to beare
    The deepe impression of so strange a sight?
    Tongue, pen, nor art, can neuer shew aright.

Amaz'd he standes, nor voyce nor body steares,
Words had no passage, teares no issue found:
For sorrow shut vp words, wrath kept in teares,
Confus'd affects each other doe confounde:
Oppress'd with griefe his passions had no bounde:
    Striuing to tell his woes, wordes would not come;
    For light cares speake, when mightie griefes are
                                                (dombe. 630

At length extremitie breakes out a way,   (attended,
Through which th'imprisoned voice with teares
Wayles out a sound that sorrowes doe bewray:
With armes a crosse and eyes to heauen bended,
Vauporing out sighes that to the skyes ascended.
    Sighes, the poore ease calamitie affords,
    Which serue for speech when sorrow wanteth
                                                (words.

O heauens (quoth he) why doe myne eyes behold,
The hatefull rayes of this vnhappy sonne?
Why haue I light to see my sinnes controld,   640

(59)

With blood of mine owne shame thus vildly donne?
How can my sight endure to looke thereon?
　　　Why doth not blacke eternall darknes hide,
　　　That from myne eyes my hart cannot abide?

What saw my life, wherein my soule might ioy?
What had my dayes, whom troubles still afflicted?
But onely this, to counterpoize annoy,
This ioy, this hope, which death hath interdicted:
This sweete, whose losse hath all distresse inflicted.
　　　This that did season all my sowre of life,　　650
　　　Vext still at home with broyles, abroade in strife.

Vext styll at home with broyles, abrode in strife,
Dissention in my blood, iarres in my bed:
Distrust at boord, suspecting still my life,
Spending the night in horror, dayes in dred;
Such life hath tyrants, and thys lyfe I led.
　　　These myseries goe mask'd in glittering showes,
　　　Which wisemen see, the vulgar little knowes.

Thus as these passions doe him ouer-whelme,
He drawes him neere my bodie to behold it:　　660
And as the Vine maried vnto the Elme
With strict imbraces, so doth he infold it;
And as he in hys carefull armes doth hold it,
　　　Viewing the face that euen death commends,
　　　On sencelesse lips, millions of kysses spends.

Pittifull mouth (quoth he) that liuing gauest
The sweetest comfort that my soule could wish:
O be it lawfull now, that dead thou hauest,
Thys sorrowing farewell of a dying kisse.
And you fayre eyes, containers of my blisse,　　670
　　　Motiues of loue, borne to be matched neuer:
　　　Entomb'd in your sweet circles sleepe for euer.

Ah how me thinks I see death dallying seekes,
To entertaine it selfe in loues sweet place:
Decayed Roses of discoloured cheekes,
Doe yet retaine deere notes of former grace:
And ougly death sits faire within her face;
    Sweet remnants resting of vermilion red,
    That death it selfe, doubts whether she be dead.

Wonder of beautie, oh receiue these plaints,   680
The obsequies, the last that I shall make thee:
For loe my soule that now already faints,
(That lou'd thee lyuing, dead will not forsake thee,)
Hastens her speedy course to ouer-take thee.
    Ile meete my death, and free my selfe thereby,
    For ah what can he doe that cannot die?

Yet ere I die, thus much my soule doth vow,
Reuenge shall sweeten death with ease of minde:
And I will cause posterity shall know,
How faire thou wert aboue all women kind.   690
And after ages monuments shall find,
    Shewing thy beauties title not thy name,
    Rose of the world that sweetned so the same.

This said, though more desirous yet to say,
(For sorrow is vnwilling to giue ouer)
He doth represse what griefe would els bewray,
Least that too much his passions might discouer:
And yet respect scarce bridles such a Louer.
    So farre transported that he knowes not whether,
    For loue and Maiestie dwell ill together.   700

Then were my funerals not long deferred,
But doone with all the rites pompe could deuise:
At *Godstow*, where my body was interred,
And richly tomb'd in honorable wise.

Where yet as now scarce any note descries
　　Vnto these times, the memory of me,
　　Marble and Brasse so little lasting be.

For those walles which the credulous deuout,
And apt-beleeuing ignorant did found:
With willing zeale that neuer call'd in doubt,　　710
That time theyr works should euer so confound,
Lye like confused heapes as vnder-ground.
　　And what their ignorance esteem'd so holy,
　　The wiser ages doe account as folly.

And were it not thy fauourable lynes,
Reedified the wracke of my decayes:
And that thy accents willingly assignes,
Some farther date, and giue me longer daies,
Fewe in this age had knowne my beauties praise.　719
　　But thus renewd, my fame redeemes some time,
　　Till other ages shall neglect thy rime.

Then when confusion in her course shall bring,
Sad desolation on the times to come:
When myrth-lesse Thames shall haue no Swan to sing,
All Musique silent, and the Muses dombe.
And yet euen then it must be known to some,
　　That once they florisht, though not cherisht so,
　　And Thames had Swannes as well as euer Po.

But heere an end, I may no longer stay thee,
I must returne t'attend at *Stigian* flood:　　730
Yet ere I goe, thys one word more I pray thee,
Tell *Delia* now her sigh may doe me good,
And will her note the frailtie of our blood.
　　And if I passe vnto those happy banks,
　　Then she must haue her praise, thy pen her thanks.

So vanisht shee, and left me to returne,
To prosecute the tenor of my woes:
Eternall matter for my Muse to mourne,
But ah the worlde hath heard too much of those,
My youth such errors must no more disclose.   740
    Ile hide the rest, and greeue for what hath beene,
    Who made me knowne, must make me liue
                                    (vnseene.

FINIS.

Mvsophilvs

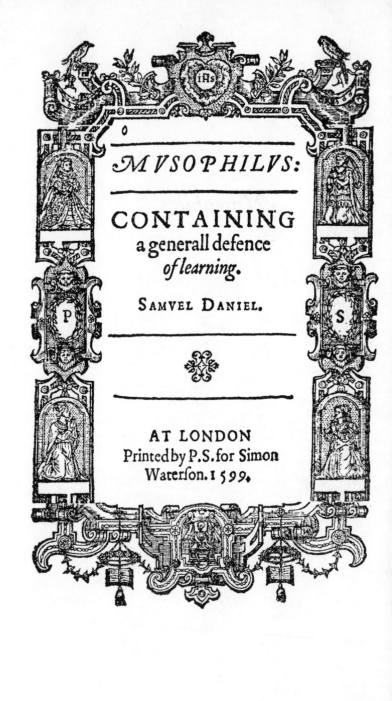

MVSOPHILVS:

CONTAINING
a generall defence
of learning.

Samvel Daniel.

AT LONDON
Printed by P.S. for Simon
Waterſon. 1 599.

To the right worthie and iudicious
fauourer of vertue, maister
Fulke Greuill.

I Do not here vpon this hum'rous Stage,
  Bring my transformed verse apparailed
With others passions, or with others rage;
With loues, with wounds, with factions furnished:
  But here present thee, onelie modelled
In this poore frame, the forme of mine owne heart:
Here to reuiue my selfe my Muse is lead   10
With motions of her owne, t'act her owne part
  Striuing to make, her now contemned arte
As faire t'her selfe as possiblie she can;
Least seeming of no force, of no desart
She might repent the course that she began,
  And, with these times of dissolution, fall
  From goodnes, vertue, glorie, fame and all.

MVSOPHILVS.

CONTAINING A
generall defence of all
learning.

PHILOCOSMVS.

FOnd man *Musophilus*, that thus dost spend
  In an vngainefull arte thy deerest daies,
Tyring thy wits and toiling to no end,
But to attaine that idle smoake of praise;
Now when this busie world cannot attend   10
Th'vntimely musicke of neglected layes.
Other delights then these, other desires
This wiser profit-seeking age requires.

Musophilus.

Friend *Philocosmus*, I confesse indeed,
I loue this sacred arte thou sett'st so light,
And though it neuer stand my life in steed,
It is inough, it giues my selfe delight,
The whiles my vnafflicted minde doth feed
On no vnholy thoughts for benefit.   20
Be it that my vnseasonable song
  Come out of time, that fault is in the time,
And I must not do vertue so much wrong
  As loue her ought the worse for others crime;
And yet I find some blessed spirits among,
  That cherish me, and like and grace my rime.
A gaine that I do more in soule esteeme
  Then al the gain of dust, the world doth craue;

(69)

And if I may attaine but to redeeme
My name from dissolution and the graue,   30
I shall haue done enough, and better deeme
T'haue liu'd to be, then to haue dyde to haue.
Short-breath'd mortalitie would yet extend
  That span of life so far forth as it may,
  And rob her fate, seeke to beguile her end
  Of some few lingring daies of after staie,
  That all this little All, might not descend
  Into the darke a vniuersall pray.
  And giue our labors yet this poore delight,
  That whẽ our daies do end they are not done;   40
  And though we die we shall not perish quite,
  But liue two liues where other haue but one.

Philocosmus.

Sillie desires of selfe-abusing man,
  Striuing to gaine th'inheritance of ayre
  That hauing done the vttermost he can
  Leaues yet perhaps but beggerie to his heir;
  Al that great purchase of the breath he wan,
  Feeds not his race, or makes his house more faire.
And what art thou the better thus to leaue   50
  A multitude of words to small effect,
  Which other times may scorn and so deceiue
  Thy promis'd name of what thou dost expect,
  Besides some viperous Creticke may bereaue
  Th'opinion of thy worth for some defect,
And get more reputation of his wit
  By but controlling of some word or sence,
  Then thou shalt honor for contriuing it,
  With all thy trauell, care and diligence;
  Being learning now enough to contradict   60
  And censure others with bold insolence.

Besides so many so confusedlie sing,
  Whose diuers discords haue the musick mar'd,
  And in contempt that mysterie doth bring,
  That he must sing alowd that will be heard;
  And the receiu'd opinion of the thing,
  For some vnhallowed strings that vildly iar'd,
Hath so vnseason'd now the eares of men,
  That who doth touch the tenor of that vaine
  Is held but vaine, and his vnreck'ned pen   70
  The title but of leuitie doth gaine.
  A poore light gaine to recompence their toile,
  That thought to get eternitie the while.
And therefore leaue the left & out-worne course
  Of vnregarded wayes, and labour how
  To fit the times with what is most in force,
  Be new with mens affections that are now;
  Striue not to run an idle counter-course
  Out from the sent of humours, men allow.
For not discreetly to compose our parts   80
  Vnto the frame of men (which we must be)
  Is to put off our selues, and make our artes
  Rebles to Nature and societie,
  Whereby we come to burie our desarts,
  In th'obscure graue of singularitie.

Musophilus.

Do not profane the worke of doing well,
  Seduced man, that canst not looke so hie
  From out that mist of earth as thou canst tell
  The wayes of right, which vertue doth descrie,   90
  That ouer-lookes the base, contemptible,
  And low-laid follies of mortalitie:
Nor meate out truth and right-deseruing prayse,
  By that wrong measure of confusion
  The vulgar foote: that neuer takes his wayes

By reason, but by imitation;
  Rowling on with the rest, and neuer way's
  The course which he should go, but what is gone.
Well were it with mankind, if what the most
  Did like were best, but ignorance will liue   100
  By others square, as by example lost;
  And man to man must th'hand of errour giue
  That none can fall alone at their owne cost,
  And all because mē iudge not, but beleeue. (boūds,
For what poore bounds haue they whom but th'earth
  What is their end whereto their care attaines,
  When the thing got relieues not, but cōfounds,
  Hauing but trauaile to succeed their paines?
  What ioy hath he of liuing that propounds
  Affliction but his end, and griefe his gaines?   110
Gath'ring, incroching, wresting, ioining to,
  Destroying, building, decking, furnishing,
  Repairing, altring, and so much a do
  To his soules toile, and bodies trauailing:
  And all this doth he little knowing who
  Fortune ordaines to haue th'inheriting.
And his faire house rais'd hie in enuies eie,
  Whose pillars rear'd perhaps on blood & wrong
  The spoyles and pillage of iniquitie,
  Who can assure it to continue long?   120
  If rage spar'd not the walls of pietie,
  Shal the profanest piles of sinne keepe strong?
How manie proude aspiring pallaces
  Haue we known made the pray of wrath and pride,
  Leuell'd with th'earth, left to forgetfulnes,
  Whilest titlers their pretended rights decide,
  Or ciuill tumults, or an orderles
  Order pretending change of some strong side?
Then where is that proude title of thy name,
  Written in yce of melting vanitie?   130

Where is thine heire left to possesse the same?
Perhaps not so well as in beggerie.
Some thing may rise to be beyond the shame
Of vile and vnregarded pouertie.
Which, I confesse, although I often striue
  To cloth in the best habit of my skill,
  In all the fairest colours I can giue;
    Yet for all that me thinks she lookes but ill,
    I cannot brooke that face, which dead-aliue
    Shewes a quicke bodie, but a buried will.   140
Yet oft we see the barres of this restraint
  Holds goodnes in, which loose wealth would let flie,
  And fruitlesse riches barrayner then want,
    Brings forth small worth from idle libertie:
    Which when disorders shal againe make scant,
    It must refetch her state from pouertie.
But yet in all this interchange of all,
  Virtue we see, with her faire grace, stands fast;
  For what hy races hath there come to fall,
    With low disgrace, quite vanished and past,   150
    Since *Chaucer* liu'd who yet liues and yet shall,
    Though (which I grieue to say) but in his last.
Yet what a time hath he wrested from time,
  And won vpon the mighty waste of daies,
  Vnto th'immortall honor of our clime,
    That by his meanes came first adorn'd with Baies,
    Vnto the sacred Relicks of whose rime
    We yet are bound in zeale to offer praise?
And could our lines begotten in this age
  Obtaine but such a blessed hand of yeeres,   160
  And scape the fury of that threatning rage,
    Which in confused clowdes gastly appeares,
    Who would not straine his trauailes to ingage,
    Whẽ such true glory should succeed his cares?
But whereas he came planted in the spring,

And had the Sun, before him, of respect;
We set in th'Autumne, in the withering,
And sullen season of a cold defect,
Must taste those soure distastes the times do bring,
Vpon the fulnesse of a cloid neglect,   170
Although the stronger constitutions shall
    Weare out th'infection of distempred daies,
    And come with glory to out-liue this fall,
    Recouring of another spring of praise,
    Cleer'd from th'oppressing humors, wherewithall
    The idle multitude surcharge their laies.
When as perhaps the words thou scornest now
    May liue, the speaking picture of the mind,
    The extract of the soule that laboured how
    To leaue the image of her selfe behind,   180
    Wherein posteritie that loue to know
    The iust proportion of our spirits may find.
For these lines are the vaines, the Arteries,
    And vndecaying life-strings of those harts
    That still shall pant, and still shall exercise
    The motion spirit and nature both imparts,
    And shall, with those aliue so sympathize
    As nourisht with their powers inioy their parts.
O blessed letters that combine in one
    All ages past, and make one liue with all,   190
    By you we do confer with who are gone,
    And the dead liuing vnto councell call:
    By you th'vnborne shall haue communion
    Of what we feele, and what doth vs befall.
Soule of the world, knowledge, without thee,
    What hath the earth that truly glorious is?
    Why should our pride make such a stir to be,
    To be forgot? what good is like to this,
    To do worthy the writing, and to write
    Worthy the reading, and the worlds delight?   200

And let th'vnnaturall and waiward race
    Borne of one wombe with vs, but to our shame,
    That neuer read t'obserue but to disgrace,
    Raise all the tempest of their powre to blame;
    That puffe of follie neuer can deface,
    The worke a happy *Genius* tooke to frame.
Yet why should ciuill learning seeke to wound
    And mangle her own members with despight?
    Prodigious wits that study to confound
    The life of wit, to seeme to know aright,   210
    As if themselues had fortunately found
    Some stand frõ of the earth beyond our sight,
    Whence ouerlooking all as from aboue,
    Their grace is not to worke, but to reproue.
But how came they plac'd in so high degree
    Aboue the reach and compasse of the rest?
    Who hath admitted them onely to be
    Free-denizons of skill, to iudge the best?
    From whom the world as yet could neuer see
    The warrant of their wit soundly exprest.   220
T'acquaint our times with that perfection
    Of high conceipt, which only they possesse,
    That we might haue things exquisitely done
    Measur'd with all their strict obseruances:
    Such would (I know) skorne a translation,
    Or bring but others labors to the presse;
    Yet oft these monster-breeding mountains wil
    Bring forth small Mice of great expected skill.
Presumption euer fullest of defects,
    Failes in the doing to performe her part;   230
    And I haue known proud words and poore effects,
    Of such indeed as do condemne this Arte:
    But let them rest, it euer hath beene knowne,
    They others vertues skorn, that doubt their owne:
And for the diuers disagreeing cordes,

Of interiangling ignorance that fill
The dainty eares, & leaue no roome for words,
The worthier mindes neglect, or pardon will;
Knowing the best he hath, he frankly foords
And skornes to be a niggard of his skill.   240

And that the rather since this short-liu'd race,
Being fatallie the sonnes but of one day,
That now with all their powre ply it apace,
To hold out with the greatest might they may
Against confusion that hath all in chace,
To make of all a vniuersall pray.

For now great *Nature* hath laid down at last
That mighty birth, wherewith so long she went
And ouerwent the times of ages past,
Here to lie in, vpon our soft content,   250
Where fruitfull she, hath multiplied so fast,
That all she hath on these times, seem'd t'haue spent.

All that which might haue many ages grac'd,
Is borne in one, to make one cloid with all;
Where plenty hath imprest a deepe distast,
Of best and worst, and all in generall:
That goodnes seems, goodnes to haue defac't,
And virtue hath to virtue giuen the fall.

For emulation, that proud nurse of wit,
Skorning to stay below or come behind,   260
Labors vpon that narrow top to sit
Of sole perfection in the highest kind;
Enuie and wonder looking after it,
Thrust likewise on the selfe same blisse to find:

And so long striuing till they can no more,
Do stuffe the place or others hopes shut out,
Who doubting to ouertake those gone before
Giue vp their care, and cast no more about;
And so in skorne leaue al as fore-possest,
And will be none where they may not be best.   270

Euen like some empty Creek that long hath lain,
　　Left or neglected of the Riuer by,　　　　(vaine,
　　Whose searching sides pleas'd with a wandring
　　Finding some little way that close did lie,
　　Steale in at first, then other streames againe
　　Second the first, then more then all supplie,
Till all the mighty maine hath borne at last
　　The glory of his chiefest powre that way,
　　Plying this new-found pleasant roome so fast
　　Till all be full, and all be at a staie;　　　　280
　　And then about, and backe againe doth cast,
　　Leauing that full to fall another way:
So feares this humorous world, that euermore
　　Rapt with the Current of a present course,
　　Runs into that which laie contemnd before;
　　Then glutted leaues the same, and fals t'a worse:
　　Now zeale holds all, no life but to adore;
　　Then cold in spirit, and faith is of no force.
　　Straight all that holie was vnhallowed lies,
　　The scattered carcasses of ruind vowes:　　　290
　　Then truth is false, and now hath blindnes eies,
　　Then zeale trusts al, now scarcely what it knows:
　　That euermore to foolish or to wise,
　　It fatall is to be seduc'd with showes.
Sacred *Religion*, mother of forme and feare,
　　How gorgeously somtimes dost thou sit deckt?
　　What pompous vestures do we make thee weare?
　　What stately piles we prodigall erect?
　　How sweet perfum'd thou art, how shining cleare?
　　How solemnly obseru'd, with what respect?　　　300
Another time all plaine, and quite threed bare,
　　Thou must haue all within and nought without,
　　Sit poorely without light, disrob'd, no care
　　Of outward grace, to amuze the poore deuout,
　　Powrelesse vnfollowed, scarcely men can spare

Thee necessary rites to set thee out.
Either truth, goodnes, vertue are not still
   The selfe same which they are, and alwaies one,
   But alter to the proiect of our will,
   Or we our actions make them waite vpon,   310
   Putting them in the liuery of our skill,
   And cast them off againe when we haue done.
You mighty Lords, that with respected grace
   Do at the sterne of faire example stand,
   And all the body of this populace
   Guide with the onely turning of your hand,
   Keepe a right course, bear vp from al disgrace,
   Obserue the point of glory to our land:
Hold vp disgraced knowledge from the ground,
   Keepe vertue in request, giue worth her due,   320
   Let not neglect with barbarous means cõfound
   So faire a good to bring in night anew.
   Be not, ô be not accessary found
   Vnto her death that must giue life to you.
Where wil you haue your vertuous names safe laid,
   In gorgeous tombes, in sacred Cels secure?
   Do you not see those prostrate heapes betraid
   Your fathers bones, and could not keepe them sure?
   And will you trust deceitfull stones faire laid:
   And thinke they will be to your honor truer?   330
No, no, vnsparing time will proudly send
   A warrant vnto wrath that with one frown
   Wil al these mock'ries of vaine glory rend,
   And make them as before, vngrac'd, vnknown,
   Poore idle honors that can ill defend
   Your memories, that cannot keepe their own.
And whereto serue that wondrous *trophei* now,
   That on the goodly plaine neare *Wilton* stands?
   That huge domb heap, that cannot tel vs how,
   Nor what, nor whence it is, nor with whose hands, 340

Nor for whose glory, it was set to shew
How much our pride mockes that of other lands?
Whereon when as the gazing passenger
   Hath greedy lookt with admiration,
   And faine would know his birth, and what he were,
   How there erected, and how long agone:
   Enquires and askes his fellow trauailer
   What he hath heard and his opinion:
And he knowes nothing. Then he turnes againe
   And looks and sighs, and then admires afresh,   350
   And in himselfe with sorrow doth complaine
   The misery of darke forgetfulnesse;
   Angrie with time that nothing should remain,
   Our greatest wonders-wonder to expresse.
Then ignorance with fabulous discourse
   Robbing faire arte and cunning of their right,
   Tels how those stones were by the diuels force
   From Affricke brought to Ireland in a night,
   And thence to Britannie by Magicke course,
   From giants hand redeem'd by *Merlins* sleight.   360
And then neare *Ambri* plac'd in memorie
   Of all those noble Britons murthred there
   By *Hengist* and his Saxon trecherie,
   Comming to parle in peace at vnaware.
   With this old Legend then credulitie
   Holdes her content, and closes vp her care:
But is antiquitie so great a liar,
   Or, do her yonger sonnes her age abuse,
   Seeing after commers still so apt t'admire
   The graue authoritie that she doth vse,   370
   That reuerence and respect dares not require
   Proofe of her deeds, or once her words refuse?
Yet wrong they did vs to presume so far
   Vpon our easie credit and delight:
   For once found false they straight became to mar

Our faith, and their owne reputation quite:
That now her truths hardly beleeued are,
And though sh'auouch y̆ right, she scarce hath right.
And as for thee, thou huge and mightie frame
That stands corrupted so with times despight,   380
And giu'st false euidence against their fame
That set thee there to testifie their right:
And art become a traitor to their name
That trusted thee with all the best they might;
Thou shalt stand still belide and slandered,
The onely gazing stocke of ignorance,
And by thy guile the wise admonished
Shal neuer more desire such heapes t'aduance,
Nor trust their liuing glorie with the dead   389
That cannot speak, but leaue their fame to chance;
Considering in how small a roome do lie
And yet lie safe, as fresh as if aliue
All those great worthies of antiquitie,
Which long foreliu'd thee, & shal long suruiue,
Who stronger tombs found for eternitie,
Then could the powres of al the earth cŏtriue.
Where they remaine these trifles to obraid
Out of the reach of spoile, and way of rage,
Though time with all his power of yeares hath laid
Long batterie, back'd with vndermining age,   400
Yet they make head onely with their own aide
And war, with his all conquering forces, wage.
Pleading the heauens prescription to be free
And t'haue a grant t'indure as long as he.

Philocosmus.

Beholde how euery man drawne with delight
Of what he doth, flatters him in his way;
Striuing to make his course seeme onely right

(80)

Doth his owne rest, and his owne thoughts betray;
Imagination bringing brauely dight   410
Her pleasing images in best aray,
With flattering glasses that must shew him faire
  And others foule; his skill and his wit best,
  Others seduc'd, deceiu'd and wrong in their;
  His knowledge right, all ignorant the rest,
  Not seeing how these minions in the aire
  Present a face of things falsely exprest,
  And that y̆ glimmering of these errors showne,
  Are but a light to let him see his owne.
Alas poore Fame, in what a narrow roome   420
  As an incaged Parrot, art thou pent
  Here amongst vs; where euẽ as good be domb
  As speake, and to be heard with no attent?
  How can you promise of the time to come
  When as the present are so negligent?
Is this the walke of all your wide renowne,
  This little point, this scarce discerned Ile,
  Thrust from y̆ world, with whõ our speech vnknown
  Made neuer any traffike of our stile.
  And is this all where all this care is showne,   430
  T'inchant your fame to last so long a while?
  And for that happier tongues haue woon so much,
  Think you to make your barbarous language such?
Poore narrow limits for so mightie paines,
  That cannot promise any forraine vent:
  And yet if here to all your wondrous vaines
  Were generally knowne, it might content:
  But lo how many reads not, or disdaines
  The labors of the chiefe and excellent.
How many thousands neuer heard the name   440
  Of *Sydney*, or of *Spencer*, or their bookes?
  And yet braue fellowes, and presume of fame
  And seem to beare downe all the world with lookes:

What then shall they expect of meaner frame,
On whose indeuours few or none scarse looks?
Do you not see these *Pamphlets*, *Libels*, *Rymes*,
These strange confused tumults of the minde,
Are growne to be the sicknes of these times,
The great disease inflicted on mankind?
Your vertues, by your follies, made your crimes, 450
Haue issue with your indiscretion ioin'd.
Schooles, arts, professions, all in so great store,
Passe the proportion of the present state,
Where being as great a number as before,
And fewer roomes them to accommodate;
It cannot be but they must throng the more,
And kicke, and thrust, and shoulder with debate.
For when the greater wittes cannot attaine
Th'expected good, which they account their right,
And yet perceiue others to reape that gaine 460
Of far inferiour vertues in their sight;
They present with the sharpe of *Enuie* straine
To wound them with reproches and despight:
And for these cannot haue as well as they, (way.
They scorne their faith should daigne to looke that
Hence discontented Sects, and Schismes arise,
Hence interwounding controuersies spring,
That feed the simple, and offend the wise,
Who know the consequence of cauilling:
Disgrace that these to others do deuise, 470
Contempt and scorne on all in th'end doth bring
Like scolding wiues reckning each others fault
Make standers by imagin both are naught.
For when to these rare dainties time admits,
All commers, all Complexions, all that will,
Where none should be let in, but choisest wits,
Whose milde discretion could comport with skill,
For when the place their humor neither fits,

Nor they the place: who can expect but ill?
For being vnapt for what they tooke in hand,   480
   And for ought else whereto they shalb'addrest
   They euen become th'incombrance of the land
   As out of ranke disordring all the rest:
   This grace of theirs to seeme to vnderstand,
   Marres all their grace to do, without their rest.
Men find that action is another thing
   Then what they in discoursing papers reade,
   The worlds affaires require in managing
   More arts then those wherin you Clearks proceed,
   Whilst timorous knowledge stands considering,   490
   Audacious ignorance hath done the deed.
   For who knowes most, the more he knows to doubt,
   The least discourse is commonly most stout.
This sweet inchaunting knowledge turnes you cleene
   Out from the fields of naturall delight,
   And makes you hide vnwilling to be seene
   In th'open concourse of a publike sight:
   This skill wherewith you haue so cunning beene,
   Vnsinewes all your powres, vnmans you quite.
Publike societie and commerce of men   500
   Require another grace, another port:
   This eloquence, these rymes, these phrases then
   Begot in shades, do serue vs in no sort,
   Th'vnmateriall swellings of your pen
   Touch not the spirit that action doth import:
A manly stile fitted to manlie eares
   Best grees with wit, not that which goes so gay,
   And commonly the gaudie liu'rie weares
   Of nice corruptions which the times do sway,
   And waites on th'humor of his pulse that beares   510
   His passions set to such a pleasing kay;
   Such dainties serue onely for stomacks weake,
   For men do fowlest when they finest speake.

Yet do I not dislike that in some wise
  Be sung the great heroycall deserts
  Of braue renowned spirits, whose exercise
  Of worthy deedes may call vp others hearts,
  And serue a modell for posterities
  To fashion them fit for like glorious parts:
  But so that all our spirits may tend hereto   520
  To make it not our grace, to say, but do.

Musophilus.

Much thou hast said, and willingly I heare,
  As one that am not so possest with loue
  Of what I do, but that I rather beare
  An eare to learne, then a toong to disproue:
  I know men must as caried in their spheare
  According to their proper motions moue.
  And that course likes them best which they are on,
  Yet truth hath certaine bounds, but falshood none.
I do confesse our limits are but small   531
  Compar'd with all the whole vaste earth beside,
  All which againe rated to that great All,
  Is likewise as a point scarcelie discride;
  So that in these respects we may this call
  A point but of a point where we abide.
But if we shall descend from that high stand
  Of ouer-looking Contemplation,
  And cast our thoughts but to, and not beyond
  This spatious circuit which we tread vpon,   540
  We then may estimate our mightie land
  A world within a world standing alone.
Where if our fame confind cannot get out,
  What, shall we then imagine it is pen'd
  That hath so great a world to walke about,
  Whose boũds with her reports haue both one end:

Why shall we not rather esteeme her stout
That farther then her owne scorne to extend?
Where being so large a roome both to do well
    And eke to heare th'applause of things well done,   550
    That farther if men shall our vertues tell
    We haue more mouthes, but not more merit won,
    It doth not greater make that which is laudable,
    The flame is bigger blowne, the fire all one.
And for the few that onely lend their eare,
    That few is all the world, which with a few
    Doth euer liue, and moue, and worke and stirre,
    This is the heart doth feele, and onely know
    The rest of all, that onely bodies beare
    Rowle vp and downe, and fill but vp the row.   560
And serue as others members not their own,
    The instruments of those that do direct.
    Then what disgrace is this not to be known
    To those know not to giue themselues respect?
    And thogh they swel with pomp of folly blown,
    They liue vngrac'd, and die but in neglect.
And for my part if onely one allow
    The care my labouring spirits take in this,
    He is to me a Theater large ynow,
    And his applause only sufficient is: 570
    All my respect is bent but to his brow,
    That is my all, and all I am is his.
And if some worthy spirits be pleased to,
    It shall more comfort breed, but not more will;
    But what if none; it cannot yet vndo
    The loue I beare vnto this holy skill:
    This is the thing that I was borne to do,
    This is my Scene, this part must I fulfill.
Let those that know not breath esteeme of wind,
    And set t'a vulgar ayre their seruile song,   580
    Rating their goodnesse by the praise they find,

Making their worth on others fits belong,
As vertue were the hyreling of the mind,
And could not liue if fame had ne'r a tongue.
Virtue. Hath that all-knowing powre that holdes within
The goodly prospectiue of all this frame,
(Where whatsoeuer is, or what hath bin,
Reflects a certaine image of the same)
No inward pleasures to delight her in,
But she must gad to seeke an almes of fame?   590
Must she like to a wanton Curtezan
Open her breasts for shew, to win her praise,
And blaze her faire bright beauty vnto man,
As if she were enamourd of his waies?
And knew not weakenes nor could rightly skan
To what defects his humorous breath obaies.
She that can tell how proud ambition
Is but a begger, and hath nought at all
But what is giuen of meere deuotion;   (thrall?
For which how much it sweats, how much it's   600
What toile it takes, and yet when all is done,
The endes in expectation neuer fall.
Shall she ioine hands with such a seruile mate,
And prostrate her faire body to commit
Folly with earth, and to defile that state
Of cleerenes, for so grosse a benefit?
Hauing reward dwelling within her gate,
And glory of her own to furnish it.
Her selfe a recompence sufficient
Vnto her selfe, to giue her owne content.   610
Ist not inough that she hath raisd so hie
Those that be hers, that they may sit and see
The earth below them, and this All to lie
Vnder their view: taking the true degree
Of the iust height of swolne mortalitie
Right as it is, not as it seemes to be,

And vndeceiued with the *paralax*
   Of a mistaking eie of passion, know
   By these mask'd outsides what the inward lacks
   Meas'ring man by himselfe not by his show,   620
   Wondring not at their rich and golden backs
   That haue poore minds, and little else to shew.
Nor taking that for them, which well they see
   Is not of them, but rather is their lode:
   The lies of fortune, wherewithall men be
   Deemed within, when they be all abroad: (& knee,
   Whose ground, whose grasse, whose earth haue cap
   Which they suppose, is on themselues bestow'd.
And thinke like *Isis* Asse, all honors are
   Giuen vnto them alone, the which are done   630
   Vnto the painted Idoll which they beare,
   That only makes them to be gazed on:
   For take away their pack and shew them bare,
   And see what beast this honor rides vpon.
Hath knowledge lent to hers the priuy kay,
   To let them in vnto the hiest stage
   Of causes, secrets, Councels; to suruay
   The wits of men, their heats, their colds, their rage,
   That build, destroy, praise, hate, say and gainesay;
   Beleeue, and vnbeleeue, all in one age.   640
And shall we trust goodnesse as it proceedes
   From that vnconstant mouth; which with one breath
   Will make it bad againe, vnlesse it feedes
   The present humor that it fauoreth?
   Shall we esteeme and reckon how it heedes
   Our works, that his own vowes vnhalloweth?
Then whereto serues it to haue been inlarg'd
   With this free manumission of the mind,
   If for all that we still continue charg'd
   With those discouered errors, which we find?   650
   As if our knowledge only were discharg'd,

Yet we our selues staid in a seruile kind.
That virtue must be out of countenance,
  If this grosse spirit, or that weake shallow brain,
  Or this nice wit, or that distemperance,
  Neglect, distast, vncomprehend, disdaine;
  When such sicke eies, can neuer cast a glance
  But through the colours of their proper staine.
Though I must needs confesse the small respect,
  That these great-seeming best of men do giue,   660
  (Whose brow begets th'inferior sorts neglect,)
  Might moue the weake irresolute to grieue:
  But stronger, see how iustly this defect
  Hath ouertooke the times wherein we liue;
That learning needs must run the common fate
  Of all things else, thrust on by her own weight,
  Comporting not her selfe in her estate
  Vnder this burthen of a selfe conceipt:
  Our own dissentious hands opening the gate
  Vnto Contempt, that on our quarrels waite,   670
Discouered haue our inward gouernment,
  And let in hard opinion to disgrace
  The generall, for some weake impotent
  That beare out their disease with a stolne face,
  Who (sillie soules) the more wit they haue spent,
  The lesse they shew'd not bettring their bad case.
And see how soone this rowling world can take
  Aduantage for her dissolution,
  Faine to get loose from this withholding stake
  Of ciuill science and discretion: 680
  How glad it would run wilde, that it might make
  One formelesse forme of one confusion?
Like tyrant *Ottomans* blindfolded state,
  Which must know nothing more but to obay:
  For this, seekes greedy ignorance t'abate
  Our number, order, liuing, forme and sway;

For this, it practises to dissipate
Th'vnsheltred troupes, till all be made awaie.
For since our fathers sinnes puld first to ground
   The pale of their disseuered dignitie,   690
   And ouerthrew that holy reuerent bound
   That parted learning and the laiety,
   And laid all flat in common to confound
   The honor and respect of pietie:
It did so much inuile the estimate
   Of th'opened and inuulgard mysteries,
   Which now reduc'd vnto the basest rate,
   Must waite vpon the *Norman* subtleties,
   Who (being mounted vp into their state)
   Do best with wrangling rudenesse sympathize.   700
And yet though now set quite behind the traine
   Of vulgar sway (and light of powre wai'd light)
   Yet would this giddy innouation faine
   Downe with it lower to abase it quite:
   And those poore remnants that do yet remain
   The spoiled marks of their deuided right:
They wholy would deface, to leaue no face
   Of reuerent distinction and degree,
   As if they waigh'd no difference in this case   709
   Betwixt *Religions* age and infancie;   (grace
   Where th'one must creepe, the other stand with
   Least turn'd to a child it ouerturned bee.
Though to pull backe th'on-running state of things,
   (Gathering corruption as it gathers daies)
   Vnto the forme of their first orderings,
   Is the best meanes that dissolution staies,
   And to go forward backward, right, men brings,
   T'obserue the line frõ whence they tooke their waies.
Yet being once gone wide, and the right way
   Not leuell to the times condition: 720
   To alter course may bring men more astray;

And leauing what was knowne to light on none,
Since euery change the reuerence doth decay
Of that which alway should continue one.
For this is that close kept *Palladium*,
Which once remou'd brings ruine euermore:
This stird makes men fore-setled to become
Curious to know what was belieu'd before:
Whilst faith disputes that vsed to be dombe,
And more men striue to talke then to adore.   730
For neuer head-strong reformation will
Rest till to th'extreame opposite it run,
And ouer-run the mean distrusted still
As being too neere of kin, to that men shun:
For good and bad, and all must be one ill,
When once there is another truth begun.
So hard it is an euen hand to beare,
In tempering with such maladies as these,
Least that our forward passions launce too near,
And make the cure proue worse then the disease:
For with the worst we will not spare the best,   741
Because it growes with that which doth displease:
And faults are easier lookt in, then redrest;
Men running with such eager violence
At the first view of errors fresh in quest,
As they to rid an inconuenience,
Sticke not to raise a mischiefe in the steed,
Which after mocks their weake improuidence:
And therefore ô make not your own sides bleed
To pricke at others, you that would amend   750
By pulling down; and thinke you can proceed
By going backe vnto the farther end,
Let stand that little Couert left behind,
Whereon your succours and respects depend.
And bring not down the prizes of the mind,
With vnder-rating of your selues so base:

You that the mighties doors do crooching find,
To sell your selues to buy a little grace,
Or waite whole months to out-bid Simonie,
For that which being got is not your place: 760
For if it were, what needed you to buy
  What was your due, your thrusting shews your shift,
  And little worth that seekes iniuriously
  A worthier from his lawfull roome to lift?
  We cannot say that you were then preferr'd,
  But that your mony was, or some worse gift.
O scattring gath'rers that without regard
  Of times to come, will to be made, vndo:
  As if you were the last of men, prepar'd
  To burie in your graues all other to.   770
  Dare you prophane that holie portion
  Which neuer sacreligious hands durst do?
Did forme-establishing deuotion,
  To maintaine a respectiue reuerence
  Extend her bountifull prouision
  With such a charitable prouidence,
  For your deforming handes to dissipate
  And make Gods due your impious expence?
No maruaile then though th'ouerpestred state
  Want roome for goodnes, if our little hold   780
  Be lessned vnto such a narrow rate
  That reuerence cannot sit, fit as it should;
  And yet what need we thus for roomes complaine,
  That shall not want void roome if this course hold:
And more then will be fill'd, for who will straine
  To get an emptie title to betray
  His hopes and trauaile for an honour vaine
  And gaine a port without support or stay?
  What need hath enuie to maligne their state
  That will themselues so kind, giue it away?   790
This makes indeed our number passe the rate

Of our prouisions; which if dealt aright
Would yeeld sufficient roome t'accommodate
More then we haue in places requisite.
The ill disposing onely doth vs set
In disaray, and out of order quite.
Whiles other gifts then of the mind shall get
Vnder our colours that which is our dues,
And to our trauailes neither benefite,
Nor grace, nor honor, nor respect accrewes: 800
This sicknes of the states soule, Learning, then
The bodies great distemprature insues.
For if that learnings roomes to learned men
Were as their heritage distributed,
All this disordred thrust would cease, for when
The fit were call'd, th'vnworthy frustrated
These would b'asham'd to seek, those to b'vnsought
And stay'ng their turn were sure they should be
Then would our drooping *Academies* brought (sped.
Againe in heart, regaine that reuerend hand   810
Of lost opinion, and no more be thought
Th'vnnecessarie furnish of the land,
Nor disincourag'd with their small esteeme,
Confus'd, irresolute, and wauering stand.
Caring not to become profound, but seeme
Contented with a superficiall skill
Which for a sleight reward inough they deem,
When th'one succeedes as well as th'other will,
Seeing shorter wayes lead sooner to their end,
And others longer trauailes thriue so ill.   820
Then would they onely labour to extend
Their now vnsearching spirits beyond these bounds
Of others powres, wherein they must be pend
As if there were besides no other grounds:
And set their bold *Plus vltra* far without
The pillers of those *Axioms* age propounds.

Discou'ring dayly more, and more about
  In that immense and boundlesse Ocean
  Of Natures riches, neuer yet found out
  Nor fore-clos'd, with the wit of any man;   830
  So far beyond the ordinarie course
  That other vnindustrious ages ran,
That these more curious times they might deuorce
  From the opinion they are linckt vnto
  Of our disable and vnactiue force,
  To shew true knowledge can both speak and do:
  Arm'd for the sharpe, which in these dayes they finde,
  With all prouisions that belong thereto.
That their experience may not come behind
  The times conceipt, but leading in their place 840
  May make men see the weapons of the mind (grace,
  Are states best strengths, and kingdoms chiefest
  And rooms of charge, charg'd ful with worth & praise
  Makes maiestie appeare with her full face,
Shining with all her beames, with all her raies,
  Vnscanted of her parts, vnshadowed
  In any darkned point: which still bewrayes
  The waine of powre, when powr's vnfurnished
  And hath not all those entire complements
  Wherewith the state should for her state be sped. 850
And though the fortune of some age consents
  Vnto a thousand errors grossely wrought,
  Which flourisht ouer with their faire euents
  Haue past for current, and good courses thought;
  The least whereof in other times againe
  Most dangerous inconueniences haue brought,
Whilst to the times, not to mens wits pertaine
  The good successes of ill manag'd deeds,
  Though th'ignorant deceiu'd with colours vaine
  Misse of the causes whence this lucke proceeds. 860
  Forreine defects giuing home-faults the way,

Make euen that weakenes somtimes well succeeds.
I grant that some vnlettered practique may
  (Leauing beyond the *Alpes* faith and respect,
  To God and man) with impious cunning sway
  The courses fore-begun with like effect,
  And without stop maintaine the turning on
  And haue his errors deemd without defect:
But when some powrefull opposition
  Shall, with a sound incountring shocke, disioint 870
  The fore-contriued frame, and thereupon
  Th'experience of the present disappoint,
  And other stirring spirits, and other hearts
  Built-huge, for action, meeting in a point;
Shall driue the world to sommon all their artes
  And all too little for so reall might,
  When no aduantages of weaker parts
  Shal beare out shallow councels from the light;
  And this sence-opening action (which doth hate
  Vnmanly craft) shall looke to haue her right.   880
Who then holds vp the glorie of the state
  (Which lettered armes, & armed letters won)
  Who shall be fittest to negotiate
  Contemn'd *Iustinian*, or else *Littleton?*
  When it shall not be held wisedome to be
  Priuately made, and publiquely vndon:
  But sound deseignes that iudgment shal decree
  Out of a true discern, of the cleare wayes
  That lie direct, with safe-going equitie
  Imbroyling not their owne & others dayes.   890
Extending forth their prouidence beyond
  The circuit of their owne particular;
  That euen the ignorant may vnderstand
  How that deceipt is but a cauiller,
  And true vnto it selfe can neuer stand,
  But stil must with her owne conclusions war.

Can truth and honestie, wherein consists
　　The right repose on earth, the surest ground
　　Of trust, come weaker arm'd into the lists,
　　Then fraud or vice, that doth it selfe confound? 900
　　Or shall presumption that doth what it lists,
　　Not what it ought, carry her courses sound?
Then what safe place out of confusion
　　Hath plain proceeding honestie to dwell?
　　What sute of grace, hath vertue to put on
　　If vice shall weare as good, and do as well?
　　If wrong, if craft, if indiscretion,
　　Act as faire parts with ends as laudable?
Which all this mightie volume of euents
　　The world, the vniuersall mappe of deedes 910
　　Strongly controwles, and proues from all discents,
　　That the directest courses best succeedes
　　When craft, wrapt still in many comberments
　　With all her cunning thriues not, though it speedes.
For should not graue and learn'd experience
　　That lookes with th'eyes of all the world beside,
　　And with all ages holdes intelligence,
　　Go safer then deceipt without a guide?
　　Which in the by-paths of her diffidence 919
　　Crossing the wayes of Right, still runs more wide:
Who will not grant? and therefore this obserue,
　　No state standes sure but on the grounds of Right,
　　Of vertue, knowledge, iudgement to preserue,
　　And all the powres of learnings requisite;
　　Though other shifts a present turne may serue,
　　Yet in the triall they will wey too light.
And do not thou contemne this swelling tide
　　And streame of words that now doth rise so hie
　　Aboue the vsuall banks, and spreads so wide
　　Ouer the borders of antiquitie: 930
　　Which I confesse comes euer amplifide

(95)

With th'abounding humours that do multiplie
And is with that same hand of happines
    Inlarg'd as vices are out of their bands;
    Yet so, as if let out but to redresse
    And calme, and sway th'affections it cõmands:
    Which as it stirres, it doth againe represse
    And brings in, th'outgone malice that withstands.
Powre aboue powres, O heauenly *Eloquence*,   939
    That with the strong reine of commanding words,
    Dost manage, guide, and master th'eminence
    Of mens affections, more then all their swords:
    Shall we not offer to thy excellence
    The richest treasure that our wit affoords?
Thou that canst do much more with one poor pen
    Then all the powres of princes can effect:
    And draw, diuert, dispose, and fashion men
    Better then force or rigour can direct:
    Should we this ornament of glorie then
    As th'vnmateriall fruits of shades, neglect?   950
Or should we carelesse come behind the rest
    In powre of wordes, that go before in worth,
    When as our accents equall to the best
    Is able greater wonders to bring forth:
    When all that euer hotter spirits exprest
    Comes bettered by the patience of the North?
And who in time knowes whither we may vent
    The treasure of our tongue, to what strange shores
    This gaine of our best glorie shal be sent,
    T'inrich vnknowing Nations with our stores?   960
    What worlds in th'yet vnformed Occident
    May come refin'd with th'accents that are ours?
Or who can tell for what great worke in hand
    The greatnes of our stile is now ordain'd?
    What powres it shall bring in, what spirits cõmand,
    What thoughts let out, what humors keep restrain'd

What mischiefe it may powrefully withstand,
And what faire ends may thereby be attain'd.
And as for Poesie (mother of this force)   (might,
  That breeds, brings forth, and nourishes this   970
  Teaching it in a loose, yet measured course,
  With comely motions how to go vpright:
  And fostring it with bountifull discourse
  Adorns it thus in fashions of delight,
What should I say? since it is well approu'd
  The speech of heauen, with whõ they haue cõmerce
  That only seeme out of themselues remou'd,
  And do with more then humane skils conuerse:
  Those nũbers wherewith heauen & earth are mou'd,
  Shew, weakenes speaks in prose, but powre in   980
Wherein thou likewise seemest to allow   (verse.
  That th'acts of worthy men shuld be preseru'd;
  As in the holiest tombes we can bestow
  Vpon their glory that haue well deseru'd,
  Wherein thou dost no other virtue show
  Then what most barbrous countries haue obseru'd:
  When all the happiest nations hitherto
  Did with no lesser glory speake then do.
Now to what else thy malice shall obiect,
  For schooles, and Arts, and their necessitie: 990
  When from my Lord, whose iudgement must direct
  And forme, and fashion my abilitie
  I shall haue got more strength: thou shalt expect
  Out of my better leasure, my reply.
And if herein the curious sort shall deeme
  My will was caried far beyond my force,
  And that it is a thing doth ill beseeme
  The function of a *Poem*, to discourse:
  Thy learned iudgement which I most esteeme
  (Worthy *Fulke Greuil*) must defend this course. 1000
By whose mild grace, and gentle hand at first

My Infant Muse was brought in open sight
From out the darkenesse wherein it was nurst,
And made to be partaker of the light;
Which peraduenture neuer else had durst
T'appeare in place, but had beene smothered quite.
And now herein incourag'd by thy praise,
Is made so bold and ventrous to attempt
Beyond example, and to trie those waies,
That malice from our forces thinkes exempt: 1010
To see if we our wronged lines could raise
Aboue the reach of lightnesse and contempt.

FINIS.

Epistles

Sir Tho: Egerton Knight,

LORD KEEPER OF THE GREAT
SEALE OF ENGLAND.

WEll hath the powreful hand of Maiestie,
   Thy worthines, and *Englands* happe beside,
Set thee in th'aidfulst roome of dignitie,
As th'*Isthmus*, these two Oceans to diuide
Of *Rigor* and confus'd *Vncertaintie*,
To keepe out th'entercourse of wrong and pride,   10
That they ingulph not vp vnsuccoured right
By th'extreame current of licencious might.

Now when we see the most combining band,
The strongest fastning of societie
Law, whereon all this frame of men doth stand,
Remaine concussed with vncertaintie,
And seeme to foster rather than withstand
Contention, and embrace obscuritie,
Onely t'afflict, and not to fashion vs,
Making her cure farre worse than the disease.   20

As if she had made couenant with Wrong,
To part the prey made on our weakenesses,
And suffred Falshood to be arm'd as strong
Vnto the combate as is Righteousnes,
Or suted her, as if she did belong
Vnto our passions, and did euen professe
Contention, as her only mystery,
Which she restraines not, but doth multiply.

Was she the same sh'is now in ages past,
Or was she lesse when she was vsed lesse?   30

(101)

And growes as malice growes, and so comes cast
Iust to the forme of our vnquietnesse?
Or made more slow, the more that strife runnes fast,
Staying t'undo vs ere she will redresse?
That th'ill shee checks seemes suffred to be ill,
When it yeelds greater gaine than goodnesse will.

Must there be still some discord mixt among
The Harmonie of men, whose moode accords
Best with Contention, tun'd t'a note of wrong,
That when war failes, peace must make war with 40
And b'arm'd vnto destruction euen as strong, (words,
As were in ages past our ciuill swordes;
Making as deepe, although vnbleeding wounds,
That when as furie failes, wisedome confounds.

If it be wisedome, and not cunning, this
Which so imbroyles the state of truth with brawles,
And wrappes it vp in strange confusednesse
As if it liu'd immur'd within the walls,
Of hideous termes fram'd out of barbarousnesse
And forraine Customes, the memorials 50
Of our subiection, and could neuer be
Deliu'red but by wrangling subtiltie.

Whereas it dwells free in the open plaine,
Vncurious, Gentile, easie of accesse:
Certaine vnto it selfe, of equall vaine,
One face, one colour, one assurednesse;
It's Falshood that is intricate, and vaine,
And needes these laborinths of subtilnesse.
For where the cunningst cou'rings most appeare
It argues still that all is not sincere. 60

Which thy cleere ey'd experience well discries,
Great *Keeper* of the state of Equitie,

Refuge of mercie, vpon whom relies
The succour of oppressed miserie:
Altar of safegarde, whereto affliction flies
From th'eger pursuite of seueritie:
Hauen of Peace, that labourst to withdraw
Iustice, from out the tempests of the Law.

And set her in a calme and euen way,
Plaine and directly leading to redresse,   70
Barring these counter-courses of delay
These wasting dilatorie processes:
Ranging into their right, and proper ray,
Errors, demurs, essoines, and trauerses,
The heads of *Hydra* springing out of death
That giues this monster, Malice, still new breath.

That what was made for the vtilitie
And good of man, might not be turn'd t'his hurt
To make him worser by his remedie,   79
And cast him downe, with what should him support:
Nor that the State of Law might loose thereby
The due respect, and reu'rence of her porte,
And seeme a trap to catch our ignorance
And to intangle our intemperance.

Since her interpretations and our deedes,
Vnto a like infinitie arise,
As be'ng a Science, that by nature breeds
Contention, strife and ambiguities:
For altercation controuersie feeds,
And in her agitation multiplies: 90
The field of *Cauell* lying all like wide,
Yealds like aduantage vnto eyther side.

inand
of
ile. Which made the graue Castillian King deuise
A prohibition, that no Aduocate

(103)

Should be conuaid to th'Indian Colonies,
Lest their new setting, shaken with debate,
Might take but slender roote, and so not rise
To any perfect growth of firme estate,
For hauing not this skill, how to contend,
Th'vnnourisht strife would quickely make an end.   100

The king of Hungarie.

So likewise did th'Hungarian, when he saw
These great Italian Bartolists, who were
Call'd in, of purpose to explane the Law,
T'imbroyle it more, and make it much lesse cleere,
Caus'd them from out his Kingdome to withdraw
With this infestious skill some other-where:

Difficultatem facit doctrina.

Whose learning rather let men farther out,
And opened wider passages of doubt.

Seeing euen Iniustice may be regulare;
And no proportion can there be betwixt   110
Our actions which in endlesse motion are
And th'Ordinances which are alwayes fixt.
Tenne thousand Lawes more, cannot reach so farre,
But Malice goes beyond, or liues immixt
So close with goodnesse, as it euer will
Corrupt, disguise or counterfeite it still.

And therefore did those glorious Monarchs, (who
Deuide with God the Stile of Maiestie
For being good, and had a care to do
The world right, and succour honestie)   120
Ordaine this sanctuarie wherevnto
Th'opprest might flie, this seate of Equitie
Whereon thy vertues sit with faire renowne,
The greatest grace and glory of the Gowne.

Which *Equitie* being the soule of Law
The life of Iustice, and the Spirite of right,

Dwell's not in written Lines, or liues in awe
Of Bookes; deafe powres that haue nor eares, nor sight:
But out of well-weigh'd circumstance doth draw
The essence of a iudgement requisite: 130
And is that Lesbian square, that building fit,
Plies to the worke, not forc'th the worke to it.

Maintaining still an equall paralell
Iust with th'occasions of humanitie,
Making her iudgements euer liable
To the respect of peace and amitie:
When surly *Law*, sterne, and vnaffable,
Cares onely but it selfe to satisfie:
And often, innocencie skarse defends,
As that which on no circumstance depends.   140

But *Equitie* that beares an euen raine
Vpon the present courses, holds in awe,
By giuing hand a little, and doth gaine
By'a gentle relaxation of the Law;
And yet inviolable doth maintaine
The end whereto all constitutions draw;
Which is the well-fare of societie
Consisting of an vpright pollicie.

Which first being by Necessitie compos'd,
ssitas Is by Necessitie maintain'd in best estate,   150
orum. Where, whenas Iustice shal be ill dispos'd
It sickens the whole body of the State:
For if there be a passage once disclos'd
That Wrong may enter at the selfe-same gate
Which serues for Right, cladde in a coate of Law,
What violent distempers may it draw?

And therefore dost thou stand to keepe the way,
And stoppe the course that malice seekes to runne

And by thy prouident *Iniunctions* stay
This neuer ending Altercation;   160
Sending contention home, to th'end men may
There make their peace, whereas their strife begun:
And free these pestred streets they vainely weare
Whom both the State, and theirs, do need elsewhere.

Lest th'humor which doth thus predominate
Conuert vnto it selfe all that it takes;
And that the law grow larger then debate,
And come t'exceede th'affaires it vndertakes:
As if the onely Science of the State
That tooke vp all our wits for gaine it makes;   170
Not for the good that thereby may be wrought
Which is not good if it be dearely bought.

What shall we thinke when as ill causes shall
Inrich men more, and shall be more desir'd
Then good, as farre more beneficiall?
Who then defends the good? who will be hir'd
A remedie for To intertaine a right, whose gaine is small?
defending ill
causes. Vnlesse the Aduocate that hath conspir'd
To pleade a wrong, be likewise made to runne
His Clients chaunce, and with him be vndunne.   180

So did the wisest nations euer striue
To binde the hands of Iustice vp so hard,
That lest she falling to prooue Lucratiue
Might basely reach them out to take reward:
Ordaining her prouisions fit to liue
Out of the publike as a publike Guard
That all preserues, and all doth entertaine,
Whose end is onely glory, and not gaine.

That eu'n the Scepter which might all command,
Seeing her s'vnpartiall, equall, regulare,   190

(106)

Was pleas'd to put it selfe into her hand;
Whereby they both grew more admired farre.
And this is that great blessing of this land,
That both the Prince and people vse one Barre,
The Prince, whose cause, (as not to be withstood)
Is neuer badde but where himselfe is good.

This is that Ballance which committed is
To thy most euen and religious hand,
Great Minister of Iustice, who by this
Shalt haue thy name, still gratious in this land: 200
This is that seale of pow're which doth impresse
Thy Acts of right, which shall for euer stand:
This is that traine of State, that pompously
Attends vpon thy reu'rent dignitie.

All glory else besides, ends with our breath,
And mens respects scarse brings vs to our graue:
But this of doing good, must out-liue Death,
And haue a right out of the right it gaue:
Though th'act but few, th'example profiteth
Thousands, that shall thereby a blessing haue.   210
The worlds respect growes not but on desarts,
Powre may haue knees, but Iustice hath our harts.

TO

The Lord Henry Howard,

ONE OF HIS MAIESTIES

PRIVIE COVNCEL.

PRaise, if it be not choice, and laide aright,
Can yeeld no lustre where it is bestowde,
Nor any way can grace the giuers Arte,
(Tho'it be a pleasing colour to delight,)
For that no ground whereon it can be shew'd
Will beare it well, but Vertue and Desart.   10

And though I might commend your learning, wit,
And happy vttrance, and commend them right,
As that which decks you much, and giues you grace,
Yet your cleere iudgement best deserueth it,
Which in your course hath caried you vpright,
And made you to discerne the truest face,
And best complexion of the things that breed
The reputation and the loue of men.
And held you in the tract of honestie
Which euer in the end we see succeed,   20
Though oft it may haue interrupted bin,
Both by the times and mens iniquitie.
For sure those actions which do fairely runne
In the right line of Honor, still are those
That get most cleane, and safest to their end,
And passe the best without confusion,
Either in those that act or else dispose,
Hauing the scope made cleere whereto they tend.
When this by-path of cunning doth s'imbroile
And intricate the passage of affaires,   30
As that they seldome fairely can get out;

(108)

But cost, with lesse successe, more care and toile
Whilst doubt and the distrusted cause impaires
Their courage, who would else appeare more stout.
  For though some hearts are builded so, that they
Haue diuers dores, whereby they may let out
Their wills abroad without disturbancie,
Int'any course, and into eu'ry way
Of humour, that affection turnes about,
Yet haue the best but one t'haue passage by.   40
  And that so surely warded with the Guarde
Of Conscience and respect, as nothing must
Haue course that way, but with the certaine passe
Of a perswasiue right, which be'ng compard
With their conceipt, must thereto answere iust,
And so with due examination passe.
  Which kind of men, rais'd of a better frame
Are meere religious, constant and vpright,
And bring the ablest hands for any'effect,
And best beare vp the reputation, fame   50
And good opinion that the Action's right,
When th'vndertakers are without suspect.
  But when the bodie of an enterprise
Shall goe one way, the face another way,
As if it did but mocke a weaker trust,
The motion being monstrous cannot rise
To any good, but falls downe to bewray
That all pretences serue for things vniust.
  Especially where th'action will allow
Apparancie, or that it hath a course   60
Concentrike with the Vniuersall frame
Of men combind, whom it concerneth how
These motions turne and intertaine their force,
Hauing their being resting on the same.
  And be it, that the vulgare are but grosse
Yet are they capable of truth, and see,

And sometimes gesse the right, and doe conceiue
The Nature of that text, that needes a glosse,
And wholy neuer can deluded be,
All may a few, few cannot all deceiue.   70
    And these strange disproportions in the traine
And course of things, do euermore proceede
From th'ill-set disposition of their minds,
Who in their actions cannot but retaine
Th'incumbred formes which do within them breede,
And which they cannot shew but in their kindes.
    Whereas the wayes and councells of the Light,
So sort with valour and with manlinesse,
As that they carry things assuredly
Vndazeling of their owne or others sight: 80
There be'ng a blessing that doth giue successe
To worthinesse, and vnto constancie.
    And though sometimes th'euent may fall amisse,
Yet shall it still haue honour for th'attempt,
When Craft begins with feare, and endes with shame,
And in the whole designe perplexed is.
Vertue, though luckelesse; yet shal skape contempt,
And though it hath not hap, it shall haue fame.

THE LADY MARGARET
COVNTESSE OF CVMBERLAND.

H E that of such a height hath built his minde,
And rear'd the dwelling of his thoughts so strong
As neither Feare nor Hope can shake the frame
Of his resolued powres, nor al the winde
Of Vanitie or Malice, pierce to wrong
His setled peace, or to disturbe the same,
What a faire seate hath he from whence hee may   10
The boundlesse wastes, and weilds of man suruay.

And with how free an eye doth he looke downe,
Vpon these lower Regions of turmoyle,
Where all these stormes of passions mainely beate
On flesh and blood, where honor, power, renowne
Are onely gay afflictions, golden toyle,
Where Greatnesse stands vpon as feeble feete
As Frailtie doth, and only great doth seeme
To little mindes, who do it so esteeme.

He lookes vpon the mightiest Monarchs warres   20
But onely as on stately robberies,
Where euermore the fortune that preuailes
Must be the right, the ill-succeeding marres
The fairest and the best-fac't enterprize:
Great Pyrat *Pompey* lesser Pyrates quailes,
Iustice, he sees, as if seduced, still
Conspires with powre, whose cause must not be ill.

He sees the face of *Right* t'appeare as manyfold
As are the passions of vncertaine man,

Who puts it in all coulours, all attires   30
To serue his ends, and make his courses hold:
He sees that let Deceit worke what it can,
Plot and contriue base wayes to high desires,
That the all-guiding Prouidence doth yet
All disappoint, and mockes this smoake of wit.

Nor is he moou'd with all the thunder crackes
Of Tyrants threats, or with the surly brow
Of power, that prowdly sits on others crimes, (checks:
Chardg'd with more crying sinnes, then those he
The stormes of sad confusion that may grow   40
Vp in the present, for the cumming times,
Appall not him, that hath no side at all
But of himselfe, and knowes the worst can fall.

Although his hart so neere allied to earth,
Cannot but pittie the perplexed State
Of troublous, and distrest mortalitie,
That thus make way vnto the ougly birth
Of their owne sorrowes, and doe still beget
Affliction vpon imbecilitie:
Yet seeing thus the course of things must run,   50
He lookes thereon, not strange, but as foredun.

And whilst distraught Ambition compasses
And is incompast, whil'st as craft deceiues
And is deceiu'd, whil'st man doth ransack man
And builds on bloud, and rises by distresse,
And th'inheritance of desolation leaues
To great expecting hopes, he lookes thereon
As from the shore of peace with vnwet eye
And beares no venture in impietie.

Thus, Madame, fares the man that hath prepar'd 60
A rest for his desires, and sees all things

Beneath him, and hath learn't this booke of man,
Full of the notes of frailtie, and compar'd
The best of glory with her sufferings,
By whom I see you labour all you can
To plant your heart, and set your thought as neere
His glorious mansion, as your powres can beare.

Which, Madame, are so soundly fashioned,
By that cleere iudgement that hath caried you
Beyond the feeble limits of your kinde,   70
As they can stand against the strongest head
Passion can make, invr'd to any hew
The world can cast, that cannot cast that minde
Out of her forme of goodnesse, that doth see
Both what the best and worst of earth can bee.

Which makes, that whatsoeuer here befalles,
You in the region of your selfe remaine,
Where no vaine breath of th'impudent molests,
That hath secur'd within the brasen walls
Of a cleere conscience, that without all staine   80
Rises in peace, in innocencie rests:
Whilst all what malice from without procures,
Shews her owne ougly heart, but hurts not yours.

And whereas none reioyce more in reuenge
Then women vse to doe, yet you well know,
That wrong is better checkt, by being contemn'd,
Then being pursu'd, leauing to him t'auenge
To whom it appertaines, wherein you show
How worthily your Clearenesse hath condemn'd
Base malediction, liuing in the darke,   90
That at the raies of goodnesse still doth barke.

Knowing the heart of man is set to be
The centre of his world, about the which

These reuolutions of disturbances
Still roule, where all th'aspects of miserie
Predominate, whose strong effects are such
As he must beare, being powrelesse to redresse,
And that vnlesse aboue himselfe he can
Erect himselfe, how poore a thing is man?

And how turmoyld they are that leuell lie   100
With earth, and cannot lift themselues from thence,
That neuer are at peace with their desires,
But worke beyond their yeares, and euen deny
Dotage her rest, and hardly will dispence
With Death: that when ability expires,
Desire liues still, so much delight they haue
To carry toile and trauaile to the graue.

Whose ends you see, and what can be the best
They reach vnto, when they haue cast the summe
And recknings of their glory, and you know   110
This floting life hath but this Port of rest,
A heart prepar'd that feares no ill to come:
And that mans greatnesse rests but in his show;
The best of all whose dayes consumed are,
Eyther in warre, or peace conceiuing warre.

This Concord (Madame) of a wel-tun'd minde
Hath beene so set by that all-working hand
Of heauen, that though the world hath done his worst,
To put it out, by discords most vnkinde,
Yet doth it still in perfect vnion stand   120
With God and Man, nor euer will be forc't
From that most sweete accord, but still agree
Equall in Fortunes inequalitie.

And this note (Madame) of your Worthines
Remaines recorded in so many Hearts

As time nor malice cannot wrong your right
In th'inheritance of Fame you must possesse,
You that haue built you by your great desarts,
Out of small meanes, a farre more exquisite
And glorious dwelling for your honoured name   130
Then all the gold of leaden mindes can frame.

S. D.

TO

The Lady Lvcie, Covn-

TESSE OF BEDFORD.

THough virtue be the same when low she stands
   In th'humble shadowes of obscuritie
  As when she either sweats in martiall bands,
Or sits in Court, clad with authoritie:
   Yet Madame, doth the strictnesse of her roome
   Greatly detract from her abilitie:
For as inwalld within a liuing tombe   10
   Her handes and armes of action, labour not;
   Her thoughts as if abortiue from the wombe,
   Come neuer borne, though happily begot.
But where she hath mounted in open sight
   An eminent, and spacious dwelling got.
   Where shee may stirre at will, and vse her might,
There is she more her selfe, and more her owne:
   There in the faire attyre of honour dight,
   She sits at ease and makes her glory knowne,   19
Applause attends her hands, her deedes haue grace,
   Her worth new-borne is straight as if ful growne,
   With such a goodly and respected face
Doth vertue looke, that's set to looke from hie,
   And such a faire aduantage by her place
   Hath state and greatnesse to doe worthily.
And therefore well did your high fortunes meete
   With her, that gracing you, comes grac't thereby,
   And well was let into a house so sweete
So good, so faire; so faire, so good a guest,
   Who now remaines as blessed in her seate,   30
   As you are with her residencie blesst.

And this faire course of knowledge whereunto
  Your studies, learned Lady, are addrest,
  Is th'onely certaine way that you can goe
Vnto true glory, to true happines:
  All passages on earth besides, are so
  Incumbred with such vaine disturbances,
As still we loose our rest, in seeking it,
  Being but deluded with apparances.
  And no key had you else that was so fit   40
T'vnlocke that prison of your Sex, as this,
  To let you out of weakenesse, and admit
  Your powers into the freedome of that blisse
That sets you there where you may ouersee
  This rowling world, and view it as it is,
  And apprehend how th'outsides do agree
With th'inward being of the things, we deeme
  And hold in our ill-cast accounts, to be
  Of highest value, and of best esteeme.
Since all the good we haue rests in the mind,   50
  By whose proportions onely we redeeme
  Our thoughts from out confusion, and do finde
The measure of our selues, and of our powres.
  And that all happinesse remaines confind
  Within the Kingdome of this breast of ours.
Without whose bounds, all that we looke on, lies
  In others Iurisdictions, others powres,
  Out of the circuit of our liberties.
All glory, honor, fame, applause, renowne,
  Are not belonging to our royalties,   60
  But t'others wills, wherein th'are onely growne.
And that vnlesse we finde vs all within,
  We neuer can without vs be our owne:
  Nor call it right our life, that we liue in:
But a possession held for others vse,
  That seeme to haue most int'rest therein.

Which we do so disseuer, parte, traduce,
Let out to custome fashion and to shew
  As we enioy but onely the abuse,
  And haue no other Deed at all to shew.   70
How oft are we constrained to appeare
  With other countenance then that we owe,
  And be our selues farre off, when we are neere?
How oft are we forc't on a clowdie hart,
  To set a shining face, and make it cleere.
  Seeming content to put our selues apart,
To beare a part of others weaknesses:
  As if we onely were compos'd by Arte,
  Not Nature, and did all our deedes addresse
T'opinion, not t'a conscience what is right: 80
  As fram'd b'example, not aduisednesse
  Into those formes that intertaine our sight. (minde,
And though Bookes, Madame, cannot make this
  Which we must bring apt to be set aright,
  Yet do they rectifie it in that kinde,
And touch it so, as that it turnes that way
  Where iudgement lies: And though we cannot finde
  The certaine place of truth, yet doe they stay,
And intertaine vs neere about the same.
  And giue the Soule the best delights that may   90
  Encheere it most, and most our spirits inflame
To thoughts of glory, and to worthy ends.
  And therefore in a course that best became
  The cleerenesse of your heart, and best commends
Your worthy powres, you runne the rightest way
  That is on Earth, that can true glory giue,
  By which when all consumes, your fame shal liue.

THE LADY ANNE

CLIFFORD.

VNto the tender youth of those faire eyes
  The light of iudgement can arise but new,
And yong the world appeares t'a yong conceit,
Whilst thorow th'vnacquainted faculties
The late inuested soule doth rawly view
Those Obiects which on that discretion waite.

  Yet you that such a faire aduantage haue,   10
Both by your birth, and happy powres t'out-go,
And be before your yeares, can fairely guesse
What hew of life holdes surest without staine,
Hauing your well-wrought hart full furnisht so
With all the images of worthinesse,

  As there is left no roome at all t'inuest
Figures of other forme but Sanctitie:
Whilst yet those cleane-created thoughts, within
The Garden of your innocencies rest,
Where are no notions of deformitie   20
Nor any dore at all to let them in.   (forth

  With so great care doth shee, that hath brought
That comely body, labour to adorne
That better parte, the mansion of your minde,
With all the richest furniture of worth,
To make y'as highly good as highly borne,
And set your vertues equall to your kinde.

  She tells you how that honour onely is
A goodly garment put on faire desarts,
Wherin the smallest staine is greatest seene,   30
And that it cannot grace vnworthinesse;

But more apparant shewes defectiue partes,
How gay soeuer they are deckt therein.

    She tells you too, how that it bounded is,
And kept inclosed with so many eyes,
As that it cannot stray and breake abroade
Into the priuate wayes of carelessenesse,
Nor euer may descend to vulgarize,
Or be below the sphere of her abode.

    But like to those supernall bodies set   40
Within their Orbs, must keep the certaine course
Of order, destin'd to their proper place;
Which only doth their note of glory get.
Th'irregulare apparances inforce
A short respect, and perish without grace.

    Being Meteors seeming hie, but yet low plac't,
    Blazing but while their dying matters last,
    Nor can we take the iust height of the minde,
But by that order which her course doth shew:
And which such splendor to her actions giues,   50
And thereby men her eminencie finde,
And thereby only do attaine to know
The Region, and the *Orbe* wherein she liues.

    For low in th'aire of grosse vncertaintie,
    Confusion onely rowles, Order sits hie.
And therefore since the dearest thing on earth,
This honour, Madame, hath his stately frame
From th'heau'nly order, which begets respect,
And that your nature, vertue, happy birth,
Haue therein highly interplac'd your name,   60
You may not runne the least course of neglect.

    For where, not to obserue, is to prophane
Your dignitie, how carefull must you be
To be your selfe, and though you may to all
Shine faire aspects, yet must the vertuous gaine
The best effects of your benignitie:

Nor must your common graces cause to fall
The price of your esteeme t'a lower rate,
Then doth befit the pitch of your estate.
    Nor may you build on your sufficiency,   70
For in our strongest partes we are but weake,
Nor yet may ouer-much distrust the same,
Lest that you come to checke it so thereby,
As silence may become worse than to speake;
Though silence women neuer ill became.
    And none, we see, were euer ouerthrowne
    By others flattery more than by their owne.
    For though we liue amongst the tongues of praise
And troopes of soothing people, that collaud
All that we do, yet 'tis within our harts   80
Th'ambushment lies, that euermore betraies
Our iudgements, when our selues be come t'applaud
Our owne abilitie, and our owne parts.
    So that we must not onely fence this forte
Of ours, against all others fraud, but most
Against our owne, whose danger is the most,
Because we lie the neerest to doe hurt,
And soon'st deceiue our selues, and soon'st are lost
By our best powres that do vs most transport.
    Such are your holy bounds, who must conuay   90
(If God so please) the honourable bloud
Of *Clifford*, and of *Russell*, led aright
To many worthy stemmes whose off-spring may
Looke backe with comfort, to haue had that good
To spring from such a branch that grew s'vpright;
    Since nothing cheeres the heart of greatnesse more
    Then th'Ancestors faire glory gone before.

Henry Wriothesly Erle

Non fert vllum ictum illæsa fœlicitas.

HE who hath neuer warr'd with misery,
   Nor euer tugg'd with Fortune and Distresse,
Hath had n'occasion nor no field to trie
The strength and forces of his worthinesse:
Those partes of iudgement which felicitie
Keepes as conceal'd, affliction must expresse;   10
And only men shew their abilities,
And what they are, in their extremities.

The world had neuer taken so full note
Of what thou arte, hadst thou not beene vndone,
And onely thy affliction hath begot
More fame then thy best fortunes could haue done:
For euer by aduersitie are wrought
The greatest workes of admiration,
And all the faire examples of renowne,
Out of distresse and misery are growne.   20

Mutius the fire, the torturs *Regulus,*
Did make the miracles of Faith and Zeale:
Exile renown'd, and grac'd *Rutilius:*
Imprisonment, and Poyson did reueale
The worth of *Socrates: Fabricius*
Pouertie did grace that Common-weale
More then all *Syllaes* riches got with strife,
And *Catoes* death did vie with *Cæsars* life.

Not to b'vnhappy is vnhappinesse;
And miserie not t'haue knowne misery: 30
For the best way vnto discretion is
The way that leads vs by aduersitie:
And men are better shew'd what is amisse,
By th'expert finger of Calamitie,
Then they can be with all that Fortune brings,
Who neuer shewes them the true face of things.

How could we know that thou could'st haue indur'd
With a reposed cheere, wrong and disgrace,
And with a heart and countenance assur'd
Haue lookt sterne Death, and Horror in the face? 40
How should we know thy soule had bin secur'd
In honest councels, and in wayes vnbase?
Hadst thou not stood to shew vs what thou wert,
By thy affliction, that describe thy heart.

It is not but the Tempest that doth shew
The Sea-mans cunning: but the field that tries
The Captaines courage: and we come to know
Best what men are, in their worst ieoperdies:
For lo, how many haue we seene to grow
To hie renowne from lowest miseries,   50
Out of the hands of death, and many a one
T'haue bin vndone, had they not bin vndone.

He that indures for what his conscience knowes
Not to be ill, doth from a patience hie
Looke, onely on the cause whereto he owes
Those sufferings, not on his miserie:
The more h'indures, the more his glory growes,
Which neuer growes from imbecilitie:
Onely the best compos'd, and worthiest harts,
God sets to act the hard'st and constant'st parts. 60

S: D.

A Defence of Ryme

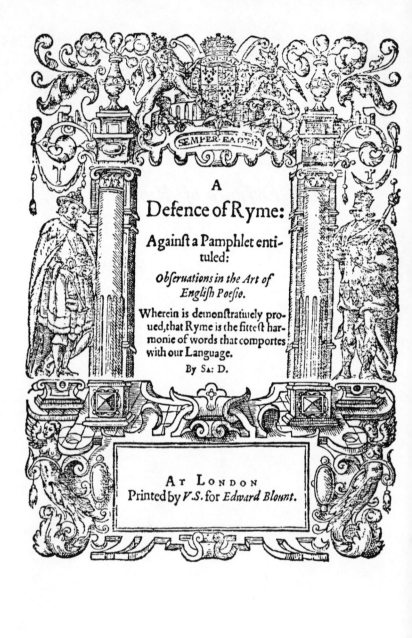

SEMPER·EADEM

A

Defence of Ryme:

Againſt a Pamphlet enti-
tuled:

*Obſeruations in the Art of
Engliſh Poeſio.*

Wherein is demonſtratiuely pro-
ued, that Ryme is the fitteſt harmonie of words that comportes
with our Language.

By Sa: D.

At London
Printed by *V.S.* for *Edward Blount.*

To all the Worthie Lo-
uers and learned Professors of Ryme,
within his Maiesties Dominions,
S. D.

Worthie Gentlemen, about a yeare since, vpon
the great reproach giuen to the Professors of
Rime, and the vse therof, I wrote a priuate letter, as
a defence of mine owne vndertakings in that kinde, to
a learned Gentleman a great friend of mine, then in
Court. Which I did, rather to confirm my selfe in
mine owne courses, and to hold him from being wonne
from vs, then with any desire to publish the same to
the world.

But now, seeing the times to promise a more regarde to the present condition of our writings, in respect of our Soueraignes happy inclination this way;
whereby wee are rather to expect an incoragement to
go on with what we do, then that any innouation
should checke vs, with a shew of what it would do in
an other kinde, and yet doe nothing but depraue: I
haue now giuen a greater body to the same Argu-
ment. And here present it to your view, vnder the
patronage of a Noble Earle, who in bloud and nature
is interessed to take our parte in this cause, with
others, who cannot, I know, but holde deare the
monuments that haue beene left vnto the world in
this manner of composition. And who I trust will
take in good parte this my defence, if not as it is my
particular, yet in respect of the cause I vndertake,
which I heere inuoke you all to protect.

Sa: D.

(127)

TO

WILLIAM HERBERT EARLE
OF PEMBROOKE.

THe Generall Custome, and vse of Ryme in this
kingdome, Noble Lord, hauing beene so long (as
if from a Graunt of Nature) held vnquestionable;
made me to imagine that it lay altogither out of the
way of contradiction, and was become so natural, as
we should neuer haue had a thought to cast it off into
reproch, or be made to thinke that it ill-became our 10
language. But now I see, when there is opposition
made to all things in the world by wordes, wee must
nowe at length likewise fall to contend for words
themselues; and make a question, whether they be
right or not. For we are tolde how that our measures
goe wrong, all Ryming is grosse, vulgare, barbarous,
which if it be so, we haue lost much labour to no purpose: and for mine owne particular, I cannot but
blame the fortune of the times and mine owne Genius
that cast me vppon so wrong a course, drawne with 20
the current of custome, and an vnexamined example.
Hauing beene first incourag'd or fram'd thereunto by
your most Worthy and Honourable Mother, receiuing the first notion for the formall ordering of those
compositions at *Wilton*, which I must euer acknow-
ledge to haue beene my best Schoole, and thereof alwayes am to hold a feeling and gratefull Memory.
Afterward, drawne farther on by the well-liking and
approbation of my worthy Lord, the fosterer of mee
and my *Muse*, I aduentured to bestow all my whole 30

powers therein, perceiuing it agreed so well, both with the complexion of the times, and mine owne constitution, as I found not wherein I might better imploy me. But yet now, vpon the great discouery of these new measures, threatning to ouerthrow the whole state of Ryme in this kingdom, I must either stand out to defend, or else be forced to forsake my selfe, and giue ouer all. And though irresolution and a selfe distrust be the most apparent faults of my na-
40 ture, and that the least checke of reprehension, if it sauour of reason, will as easily shake my resolution as any mans liuing: yet in this case I know not how I am growne more resolued, and before I sinke, willing to examine what those powers of iudgement are, that must beare me downe, and beat me off from the station of my profession, which by the law of nature I am set to defend.

And the rather for that this detractor (whose commendable Rymes albeit now himselfe an enemy to
50 ryme, haue giuen heretofore to the world the best notice of his worth) is a man of faire parts, and good reputation, and therefore the reproach forcibly cast from such a hand may throw downe more at once then the labors of many shall in long time build vp againe, specially vpon the slippery foundation of opinion, and the worlds inconstancy, which knowes not well what it would haue, and:

> *Discit enim citius, meminitque libentius illud*
> *Quod quis deridet quam quod probat & veneratur.*

60 And he who is thus, become our vnkinde aduersarie, must pardon vs if we be as iealous of our fame and reputation, as hee is desirous of credite by his new-old arte, and must consider that we cannot, in a thing that concernes vs so neere, but haue a feeling of the wrong done, wherein euery Rymer in this vniuer-

sall Iland as well as my selfe, stands interressed. So
that if his charitie had equally drawne with his learning hee would haue forborne to procure the enuie of
so powerfull a number vpon him, from whom he cannot but expect the returne of a like measure of blame,   70
and onely haue made way to his owne grace, by the
proofe of his abilitie, without the disparaging of vs,
who would haue bin glad to haue stood quietly by
him, & perhaps commended his aduenture, seeing
that euermore of one science an other may be borne,
& that these Salies made out of the quarter of our set
knowledges, are the gallant proffers onely of attemp-
tiue spirits, and commendable though they worke no
other effect than make a Brauado: and I know it
were *Indecens, & morosum nimis, alienæ industriæ*,   80
modum ponere. We could well haue allowed of his
numbers had he not disgraced our Ryme; Which both
Custome and Nature doth most powerfully defend.
Custome that is before all Law, Nature that is aboue
all Arte. Euery language hath her proper number or
measure fitted to vse and delight, which, Custome in-
tertaining by the allowance of the Eare, doth inden-
ize, and make naturall. All verse is but a frame of
wordes confinde within certaine measure; differing
from the ordinarie speach, and introduced, the better   90
to expresse mens conceipts, both for delight and
memorie. Which frame of wordes consisting of *Rith-
mus* or *Metrum*, Number or Measure, are disposed
into diuers fashions, according to the humour of the
Composer and the set of the time; And these *Rhythmi*
as *Aristotle* saith are familiar amongst all Nations,
and *è naturali & sponte fusa compositione:* And they
fall as naturally already in our language as euer Art
can make them; being such as the Eare of it selfe doth
marshall in their proper roomes, and they of them-   100

selues will not willingly be put out of their ranke; and
that in such a verse as best comports with the Nature
of our language. And for our Ryme (which is an excellencie added to this worke of measure, and a Harmonie, farre happier than any proportion Antiquitie
could euer shew vs) dooth adde more grace, and hath
more of delight than euer bare numbers, howsoeuer
they can be forced to runne in our slow language, can
possibly yeeld. Which, whether it be deriu'd of
110 *Rhythmus*, or of *Romance* which were songs the *Bards
& Druydes* about Rymes vsed, & therof were caled
Remensi, as some Italians hold; or howsoeuer, it is
likewise number and harmonie of words, consisting of
an agreeing sound in the last silables of seuerall
verses, giuing both to the Eare an Eccho of a delightfull report & to the Memorie a deeper impression of
what is deliuered therein. For as Greeke and Latine
verse consists of the number and quantitie of sillables, so doth the English verse of measure and ac-
120 cent. And though it doth not strictly obserue long
and short sillables, yet it most religiously respects the
accent: and as the short and the long make number,
so the Acute and graue accent yeelde harmonie: And
harmonie is likewise number, so that the English
verse then hath number, measure and harmonie in
the best proportion of Musike. Which being more
certain & more resounding, works that effect of motion with as happy successe as either the Greek or
Latin. And so naturall a melody is it, & so vniuersall
130 as it seems to be generally borne with al the nations
of the world, as an hereditary eloquence proper to all
mankind. The vniuersallitie argues the generall
power of it: for if the Barbarian vse it, then it shews
that it swais th'affection of the Barbarian, if ciuil
nations practise it, it proues that it works vpon the

harts of ciuil nations: If all, then that it hath a power in nature on all. *Georgieuez de Turcarum moribus,* hath an example of the Turkish Rymes iust of the measure of our verse of eleuen sillables, in feminine Ryme: neuer begotten I am perswaded by any exam- 140 ple in *Europe,* but borne no doubt in *Scythia,* and brought ouer *Caucasus* and *Mount Taurus.* The Sclauonian and Arabian tongs acquaint a great part of *Asia* and *Affrique* with it, the Moscouite, Polack, Hungarian, German, Italian, French, and Spaniard vse no other harmonie of words. The Irish, Briton, Scot, Dane, Saxon, English, and all the Inhabiters of this Iland, either haue hither brought, or here found the same in vse. And such a force hath it in nature, or so made by nature, as the Latine numbers notwith- 150 standing their excellencie, seemed not sufficient to satitsfie the eare of the world thereunto accustomed, without this Harmonicall cadence: which made the most learned of all nations labour with exceeding trauaile to bring those numbers likewise vnto it: which many did with that happinesse, as neither their puritie of tongue, nor their materiall contemplations are thereby any way disgraced, but rather deserue to be reuerenced of all gratefull posteritie, with the due regard of their worth. And for *Schola Salerna,* and 160 those *Carmina Prouerbialia,* who finds not therein more precepts for vse, concerning diet, health, and conuersation, then *Cato, Theognes,* or all the Greekes and Latines can shew vs in that kinde of teaching: and that in so few words, both for delight to the eare, and the hold of memorie, as they are to be imbraced of all modest readers that studie to know and not to depraue.

Me thinkes it is a strange imperfection, that men should thus ouer-runne the estimation of good things 170 with so violent a censure, as though it must please none else, because it likes not them. Whereas *Oportet arbitratores esse non contradictores eos qui verum iudicaturi sunt*, saith *Arist.* though he could not obserue it himselfe. And milde Charitie tells vs:

— non ego paucis
Offendor maculis quas aut incuria fudit
Aut humana parum cauet natura. For all men haue their errors, and we must take the best of their 180 powers, and leaue the rest as not appertaining vnto vs.

Ill customes are to be left, I graunt it: but I see not howe that can be taken for an ill custome, which nature hath thus ratified, all nations receiued, time so long confirmed, the effects such as it performes those offices of motion for which it is imployed; delighting the eare, stirring the heart, and satisfying the iudgement in such sort as I doubt whether euer single numbers will do in our Climate, if they shew no more 190 worke of wonder then yet we see. And if euer they prooue to become any thing, it must be by the approbation of many ages that must giue them their strength for any operation, or before the world will feele where the pulse, life, and enargie lies, which now we are sure where to haue in our Rymes, whose knowne frame hath those due staies for the minde, those incounters of touch as makes the motion certaine, though the varietie be infinite. Nor will the Generall sorte, for whom we write (the wise being 200 aboue bookes) taste these laboured measures but as an orderly prose when wee haue all done. For this kinde acquaintance and continuall familiaritie euer had betwixt our eare and this cadence, is growne to so intimate a friendship, as it will nowe hardly euer be brought to misse it. For be the verse neuer so

good, neuer so full, it seemes not to satisfie nor breede
that delight as when it is met and combined with a
like sounding accent. Which seemes as the iointure
without which it hangs loose, and cannot subsist, but
runnes wildely on, like a tedious fancie without a 210
close: suffer then the world to inioy that which it
knowes, and what it likes. Seeing that whatsoeuer
force of words doth mooue, delight and sway the affections of men, in what Scythian sorte soeuer it be
disposed or vttered: that is true number, measure,
eloquence, and the perfection of speach: which I said,
hath as many shapes as there be tongues or nations
in the world, nor can with all the tyrannicall Rules of
idle Rhetorique be gouerned otherwise then custome,
and present obseruation will allow. And being now 220
the trym, and fashion of the times, to sute a man
otherwise cannot but giue a touch of singularity, for
when hee hath all done, hee hath but found other
clothes to the same body, and peraduenture not so
fitting as the former. But could our Aduersary hereby set vp the musicke of our times to a higher note of
iudgement and discretion, or could these new lawes
of words better our imperfections, it were a happy attempt; but when hereby we shall but as it were
change prison, and put off these fetters to receiue 230
others, what haue we gained, as good still to vse
ryme and a little reason, as neither ryme nor reason,
for no doubt as idle wits will write, in that kinde, as
do now in this, imitation wil after, though it breake
her necke. *Scribimus indocti doctique poemata pas-
sim.* And this multitude of idle writers can be no disgrace to the good, for the same fortune in one proportion or other is proper in a like season to all States
in their turne: and the same vnmeasureable conflu-
ence of Scriblers hapned, when measures were most 240

in vse among the Romanes, as we finde by this reprehension,

Mutauit mentem populus leuis, & calet vno
Scribendi studio, pueri, patrésque seueri,
Fronde comas vincti cœnant, & carmina dictant.

So that their plentie seemes to haue bred the same
waste and contempt as ours doth now, though it had
not power to disvalew what was worthy of posteritie,
nor keep backe the reputation of excellencies, de-
250 stined to continue for many ages. For seeing it is
matter that satisfies the iudiciall, appeare it in what
habite it will, all these pretended proportions of
words, howsoeuer placed, can be but words, and peraduenture serue but to embroyle our vnderstanding,
whilst seeking to please our eare, we inthrall our iudgement: to delight an exterior sense, wee smoothe vp a
weake confused sense, affecting sound to be vnsound,
and all to seeme *Seruum pecus*, onely to imitate the
Greekes and Latines, whose felicitie, in this kind,
260 might be something to themselues, to whome their
owne *idioma* was naturall, but to vs it can yeeld no
other commoditie then a sound. We admire them
not for their smooth-gliding words, nor their measures, but for their inuentions: which treasure, if it
were to be found in Welch, and Irish, we should hold
those languages in the same estimation, and they
may thanke their sword that made their tongues so
famous and vniuersall as they are. For to say truth,
their Verse is many times but a confused deliuerer of
270 their excellent conceits, whose scattered limbs we are
faine to looke out and ioyne together, to discerne the
image of what they represent vnto vs. And euen the
Latines, who professe not to be so licentious as the
Greekes, shew vs many times examples but of strange
crueltie, in torturing and dismembring of wordes in

the middest, or disioyning such as naturally should
be married and march together, by setting them as
farre asunder, as they can possibly stand: that sometimes, vnlesse the kind reader, out of his owne good
nature, wil stay them vp by their measure, they will 280
fall downe into flatte prose, and sometimes are no
other indeede in their naturall sound: and then
againe, when you finde them disobedient to their
owne Lawes, you must hold it to be *licentia poetica*,
and so dispensable. The striuing to shew their
changable measures in the varietie of their Odes, haue
beene very painefull no doubt vnto them, and forced
them thus to disturbe the quiet streame of their
wordes, which by a naturall succession otherwise de-
sire to follow in their due course.   290

But such affliction doth laboursome curiositie still
lay vpon our best delights (which euer must be made
strange and variable) as if Art were ordained to afflict Nature, and that we could not goe but in fetters.
Euery science, euery profession, must be so wrapt vp
in vnnecessary intrications, as if it were not to fashion, but to confound the vnderstanding, which makes
me much to distrust man, and feare that our presumption goes beyond our abilitie, and our Curiositie
is more than our Iudgement: laboring euer to seeme 300
to be more than we are, or laying greater burthens
vpon our mindes, then they are well able to beare,
because we would not appeare like other men.

And indeed I haue wished there were not that
multiplicitie of Rymes as is vsed by many in Sonets,
which yet we see in some so happily to succeed, and
hath beene so farre from hindering their inuentions,
as it hath begot conceit beyond expectation, and com-
parable to the best inuentions of the world: for sure in
an eminent spirit whome Nature hath fitted for that 310

mysterie, Ryme is no impediment to his conceit, but rather giues him wings to mount and carries him, not out of his course, but as it were beyond his power to a farre happier flight. Al excellencies being sold vs at the hard price of labour, it followes, where we bestow most thereof, we buy the best successe: and Ryme being farre more laborious then loose measures (whatsoeuer is obiected) must needs, meeting with wit and industry, breed greater and worthier effects in our language. So that if our labours haue wrought out a manumission from bondage, and that wee goe at libertie, notwithstanding these ties, wee are no longer the slaues of Ryme, but we make it a most excellent instrument to serue vs. Nor is this certaine limit obserued in Sonnets, any tyrannicall bounding of the conceit, but rather a reducing it in *girum*, and a iust forme, neither too long for the shortest proiect, nor too short for the longest, being but onely imployed for a present passion. For the body of our imagination, being as an vnformed *Chaos* without fashion, without day, if by the diuine power of the spirit it be wrought into an Orbe of order and forme, is it not more pleasing to Nature, that desires a certaintie, and comports not with that which is infinite, to haue these clozes, rather than, not to know where to end, or how farre to goe, especially seeing our passions are often without measure: and wee finde the best of the latines many times, either not concluding, or els otherwise in the end then they began. Besides, is it not most delightfull to see much excellently ordred in a small roome, or little, gallantly disposed and made to fill vp a space of like capacitie, in such sort, that the one would not appeare so beautifull in a larger circuite, nor the other do well in a lesse: which often we find to be so, according to the powers of nature, in the worke-man. And these limited proportions, and rests of Stanzes: consisting of 6. 7. or 8. lines are of that happines, both for the disposition of the matter, the apt planting the sentence where it may best stand to hit, the certaine close of delight with the full body of a 350 iust period well carried, is such, as neither the Greekes or Latines euer attained vnto. For their boundlesse running on, often so confounds the Reader, that hauing once lost himselfe, must either giue off vnsatisfied, or vncertainely cast backe to retriue the escaped sence, and to find way againe into his matter.

Me thinkes we should not so soone yeeld our consents captiue to the authoritie of Antiquitie, vnlesse we saw more reason: all our vnderstandings are not to be built by the square of *Greece* and *Italie*. We are 360 the children of nature as well as they, we are not so placed out of the way of iudgement, but that the same Sunne of Discretion shineth vppon vs, wee haue our portion of the same vertues as well as of the same vices, *Et Catilinam Quocunque in populo videas, quocunque sub axe.* Time and the turne of things bring about these faculties according to the present estimation: and, *Res temporibus non tempora rebus seruire opportet.* So that we must neuer rebell against vse: *Quem penes arbitrium est, & vis & norma lo-* 370 *quendi.* It is not the obseruing of *Trochaicques* nor their *Iambicques*, that wil make our writings ought the wiser: All their Poesie, all their Philosophie is nothing, vnlesse we bring the discerning light of conceipt with vs to apply it to vse. It is not bookes, but onely that great booke of the world, and the all-ouerspreading grace of heauen that makes men truely iudiciall. Nor can it be but a touch of arrogant ignorance, to hold this or that nation Barbarous, these or those times grosse, considering how this manifold 380

creature man, wheresoeuer hee stand in the world, hath alwayes some disposition of worth, intertaines the order of societie, affects that which is most in vse, and is eminent in some one thing or other, that fits his humour and the times. The Grecians held all other nations barbarous but themselues, yet *Pirrhus* when he saw the well ordered marching of the Romanes, which made them see their presumptuous errour, could say it was no barbarous maner of proceed-
390 ing. The *Gothes*, *Vandales* and *Longobards*, whose comming downe like an inundation ouerwhelmed, as they say, al the glory of learning in *Europe*, haue yet left vs still their lawes and customes, as the originalls of most of the prouinciall constitutions of Christendome; which well considered with their other courses of gouernement, may serue to cleere them from this imputation of ignorance. And though the vanquished neuer yet spake well of the Conquerour: yet euen thorow the vnsound couerings of malediction appeare
400 those monuments of trueth, as argue wel their worth and proues them not without iudgement, though without Greeke and Latine.

Will not experience confute vs, if wee shoulde say the state of *China*, which neuer heard of Anapestiques, Trochies, and Tribracques, were grosse, barbarous, and vnciuile? And is it not a most apparant ignorance, both of the succession of learning in *Europe*, and the generall course of things, *to say, that all lay pittifully deformed in those lacke-learning times*
410 *from the declining of the Romane Empire, till the light of the Latine tongue was reuiued by* Rewcline, Erasmus *and* Moore. When for three hundred yeeres before them about the comming downe of *Tamburlaine* into *Europe*, *Franciscus Petrarcha* (who then no doubt likewise found whom to imitate) shewed all the best

notions of learning, in that degree of excellencie, both
in Latin, Prose and Verse, and in the vulgare Italian,
as all the wittes of posteritie haue not yet much ouer-
matched him in all kindes to this day: his great Volumes written in Moral Philosophie, shew his infinite 420
reading, and most happy power of disposition: his
twelue Æglogues, his *Affrica* containing nine Bookes
of the last Punicke warre, with his three Bookes of
Epistles in Latine verse, shew all the transformations
of wit and inuention, that a Spirite naturally borne
to the inheritance of Poetrie & iudiciall knowledge
could expresse: All which notwithstanding wrought
him not that glory & fame with his owne Nation, as
did his Poems in Italian, which they esteeme aboue
al whatsoeuer wit could haue inuented in any other 430
forme then wherein it is: which questionles they wil
not change with the best measures, Greeks or Latins
can shew them; howsoeuer our Aduersary imagines.
Nor could this very same innouation in Verse, begun
amongst them by *C. Tolomæi*, but die in the attempt,
and was buried as soone as it came borne, neglected
as a prodigious & vnnaturall issue amongst them:
nor could it neuer induce *Tasso* the wonder of *Italy*,
to write that admirable Poem of *Ierusalem*, compar-
able to the best of the ancients, in any other forme 440
then the accustomed verse. And with *Petrarch* liued
his scholer *Boccacius*, and neere about the same time,
Iohannis Rauenensis, and from these *tanquam ex equo
Troiano*, seemes to haue issued all those famous
Italian Writers, *Leonardus Aretinus*, *Laurentius
Valla*, *Poggius*, *Blondus*, and many others. Then
Emanuel Chrysolaras a Constantinopolitan gentleman, renowmed for his learning and vertue, being
imployed by *Iohn Paleologus* Emperour of the East,
to implore the ayde of christian Princes, for the suc- 450

couring of perishing *Greece:* and vnderstanding in the meane time, how *Baiazeth* was taken prisoner by *Tamburlan,* and his country freed from danger, stayed still at *Venice,* and there taught the Greeke tongue, discontinued before, in these parts the space of seauen hundred yeeres. Him followed *Bessarion, George Trapezantius, Theodore Gaza,* & others, transporting Philosophie beaten by the Turke out of *Greece* into christendome. Hereupon came that mightie conflu-
460 ence of Learning in these parts, which returning, as it were *per postliminium,* and heere meeting then with the new inuented stampe of Printing, spread it selfe indeed in a more vniuersall sorte then the world euer heeretofore had it. When *Pomponius Lætus, AEneas Syluius, Angelus Politianus, Hermolaus Barbarus, Iohannes Picus de Mirandula* the miracle & Phœnix of the world, adorned *Italie,* and wakened vp other Nations likewise with this desire of glory, long before it brought foorth, *Rewclen, Erasmus,* and
470 *Moore,* worthy men I confesse, and the last a great ornament to this land, and a Rymer. And yet long before all these, and likewise with these, was not our Nation behind in her portion of spirite and worth-inesse, but concurrent with the best of all this lettered worlde: witnesse venerable *Bede,* that flourished a-boue a thousand yeeres since: *Aldelmus Durotelmus* that liued in the yeere 739. of whom we finde this commendation registred: *Omnium Poetarum sui temporis facilè primus, tantæ eloquentiæ, maiestatis &*
480 *eruditionis homo fuit, vt nunquam satis admirari possim vnde illi in tam barbara ac rudi ætate facundia accreuerit, vsque adeo omnibus numeris tersa, elegans & rotunda, versus edidit cum antiquitate de palma contendentes.* Witnesse *Iosephus Deuonius,* who wrote *de bello Troiano,* in so excellent manner, and so neere resem-

bling Antiquitie, as Printing his Worke beyond the Seas, they haue ascribed it to *Cornelius Nepos*, one of the Ancients.

What should I name *Walterus Mape*, *Gulielmus Nigellus*, *Geruasius Tilburiensis*, *Bracton*, *Bacon*, *Ockam*, and an infinite Catalogue of excellent men, most of them liuing about foure hundred yeares since, and haue left behinde them monuments of most profound iudgement and learning in all sciences. So that it is but the clowds gathered about our owne iudgement that makes vs thinke all other ages wrapt vp in mists, and the great distance betwixt vs, that causes vs to imagine men so farre off, to be so little in respect of our selues. We must not looke vpon the immense course of times past, as men ouer-looke spacious and wide countries, from off high Mountaines and are neuer the neere to iudge of the true Nature of the soyle, or the particular syte and face of those territories they see. Nor must we thinke, viewing the superficiall figure of a region in a Mappe that wee know strait the fashion and place as it is. Or reading an Historie (which is but a Mappe of men, and dooth no otherwise acquaint vs with the true Substance of Circumstances, than a superficiall Card dooth the Seaman with a Coast neuer seene, which alwayes prooues other to the eye than the imagination forecast it) that presently wee know all the world, and can distinctly iudge of times, men and maners, iust as they were. When the best measure of man is to be taken by his owne foote, bearing euer the neerest proportion to himselfe, and is neuer so farre different and vnequall in his powers, that he hath all in perfection at one time, and nothing at an other. The distribution of giftes are vniuersall, and all seasons hath them in some sort. We must not thinke, but that there were

490

500

510

520

Scipioes, *Cæsars*, *Catoes* and *Pompeies*, borne elsewhere then at *Rome*, the rest of the world hath euer
had them in the same degree of nature, though not of
state. And it is our weakenesse that makes vs mistake, or misconceiue in these deliniations of men the
true figure of their worth. And our passion and beliefe is so apt to leade vs beyond truth, that vnlesse
we try them by the iust compasse of humanitie, and
as they were men, we shall cast their figures in the
530 ayre when we should make their models vpon Earth.
It is not the contexture of words, but the effects of
Action that giues glory to the times: we finde they
had *mercurium in pectore* though not *in lingua*, and
in all ages, though they were not Ciceronians, they
knew the Art of men, which onely is, *Ars Artium*, the
great gift of heauen, and the chiefe grace and glory on
earth, they had the learning of Gouernement, and
ordring their State, Eloquence inough to shew their
iudgements. And it seemes the best times followed
540 *Lycurgus* councell: *Literas ad vsum saltem discebant,
reliqua omnis disciplina erat, vt pulchre parerent vt
labores perferrent &c.* Had not vnlearned *Rome* laide
the better foundation, and built the stronger frame of
an admirable state, eloquent *Rome* had confounded it
vtterly, which we saw, ranne the way of all confusion,
the plaine course of dissolution in her greatest skill:
and though she had not power to vndoe her selfe, yet
wrought she so that she cast her selfe quite away
from the glory of a common-wealth, and fell vpon
550 that forme of state she euer most feared and abhorred
of all other: and then scarse was there seene any
shadowe of pollicie vnder her first Emperours, but the
most horrible and grosse confusion that could bee
conceued, notwithstanding it stil indured, preseruing
not only a Monarchie, locked vp in her own limits,

but therewithall held vnder her obedience, so many Nations so farre distant, so ill affected, so disorderly commanded & vniustly conquerd, as it is not to be attributed to any other fate but to the first frame of that commonwealth, which was so strongly ioynted and with such infinite combinations interlinckt, as one naile or other euer held vp the Maiestie thereof. There is but one learning, which *omnes gentes habent scriptum in cordibus suis,* one and the selfe-same spirit that worketh in all. We haue but one body of Iustice, one body of Wisedome throughout the whole world, which is but apparaled according to the fashion of euery nation.

Eloquence and gay wordes are not of the Substance of wit, it is but the garnish of a nice time, the Ornaments that doe but decke the house of a State, & *imitatur publicos mores:* Hunger is as well satisfied with meat serued in pewter as siluer. Discretion is the best measure, the rightest foote in what habit soeuer it runne. *Erasmus, Rewcline* and *More,* brought no more wisdome into the world with all their new reuiued wordes then we finde was before, it bred not a profounder Diuine than Saint *Thomas,* a greater Lawyer than *Bartolus,* a more accute Logician than *Scotus:* nor are the effects of all this great amasse of eloquence so admirable or of that consequence, but that *impexa illa antiquitas* can yet compare with them. Let vs go no further, but looke vpon the wonderfull Architecture of this state of *England,* and see whether they were deformed times, that could giue it such a forme. Where there is no one the least piller of Maiestie, but was set with most profound iudgement and borne vp with the iust conueniencie of Prince and people. No Court of Iustice, but laide by the Rule and Square of Nature, and the best of the best commonwealths that euer were in the world. So strong and substantial, as it hath stood against al the storms of factions, both of beliefe & ambition, which so powerfully beat vpon it, and all the tempestuous alterations of humorous times whatsoeuer. Being continually in all ages furnisht with spirites fitte to maintaine the maiestie of her owne greatnes, and to match in an equall concurrencie all other kingdomes round about her with whome it had to incounter. But this innouation, like a Viper, must euer make way into the worlds opinion, thorow the bowelles of her owne breeding, & is alwayes borne with reproch in her mouth; the disgracing others is the best grace it can put on, to winne reputation of wit, and yet is it neuer so wise as it would seeme, nor doth the world euer get so much by it, as it imagineth: which being so often deceiued, and seeing it neuer performes so much as it promises, me thinkes men should neuer giue more credite vnto it. For, let vs change neuer so often, wee can not change man, our imperfections must still runne on with vs. And therefore the wiser Nations haue taught menne alwayes to vse, *Moribus legibusque presentibus etiamsi deteriores sint.* The Lacedemonians, when a Musitian, thincking to winne him-selfe credite by his new inuention, and be before his fellowes, had added one string more to his Crowde, brake his fiddle, and banished him the Cittie, holding the Innouator, though in the least things, dangerous to a publike societie. It is but a fantastike giddinesse to forsake the way of other men, especially where it lies tollerable: *Vbi nunc est respublica, ibi simus potius quam dum illam veterem sequimur, simus in nulla.* But shal we not tend to perfection? Yes, and that euer best by going on in the course we are in, where we haue aduantage, being so farre onward, of him that is but now setting forth. For we shall neuer proceede, if wee be euer beginning, nor arriue at any certayne Porte, sayling with all windes that blow: *Non conualescit planta quæ sæpius transfertur*, and therefore let vs hold on in the course wee haue vnder- 630 taken, and not still be wandring. Perfection is not the portion of man, and if it were, why may wee not as well get to it this way as an other? and suspect these great vndertakers, lest they haue conspired with enuy to betray our proceedings, and put vs by the honor of our attempts, with casting vs backe vpon an other course, of purpose to ouerthrow the whole action of glory when we lay the fairest for it, and were so neere our hopes? I thanke God that I am none of these great Schollers, if thus their hie knowledges doe but 640 giue them more eyes to looke out into vncertaintie and confusion, accounting my selfe, rather beholding to my ignorance, that hath set me in so lowe an vnder-roome of conceipt with other men, and hath giuen me as much distrust, as it hath done hope, daring not aduenture to goe alone, but plodding on the plaine tract I finde beaten by Custome and the Time, con-tenting me with what I see in vse. And surely mee thinkes these great wittes should rather seeke to adorne, than to disgrace the present, bring something 650 to it, without taking from it what it hath. But it is euer the misfortune of Learning, to be wounded by her owne hand. *Stimulos dat emula virtus*, and when there is not abilitie to match what is, malice wil finde out ingines, either to disgrace or ruine it, with a per-uerse incounter of some new impression: and which is the greatest misery, it must euer proceed from the powers of the best reputation, as if the greatest spirites were ordained to indanger the worlde, as the grosse are to dishonour it, and that we were to expect 660

ab optimis periculum, à pessimis dedecus publicum.
Emulation the strongest pulse that beates in high
mindes, is oftentimes a winde, but of the worst effect:
For whilst the Soule comes disappoynted of the obiect
it wrought on, it presently forges an other, and euen
cozins it selfe, and crosses all the world, rather than
it wil stay to be vnder hir desires, falling out with all
it hath, to flatter and make faire that which it would
haue. So that it is the ill successe of our longings that
670 with *Xerxes* makes vs to whippe the Sea, and send a
cartel of defiance to mount *Athos:* and the fault laide
vpon others weakenesse, is but a presumptuous opinion of our owne strength, who must not seeme to be
maistered. But had our Aduersary taught vs by his
owne proceedings, this way of perfection, and therein
fram'd vs a Poeme of that excellencie as should haue
put downe all, and beene the maister-peece of these
times, we should all haue admired him. But to depraue the present forme of writing, and to bring
680 vs nothing but a few loose and vncharitable Epi-
grammes, and yet would make vs belieue those numbers were come to raise the glory of our language,
giueth vs cause to suspect the performance, and to
examine whether this new Arte, *constat sibi,* or, *aliquid*
sit dictum quod non sit dictum prius.

First we must heere imitate the Greekes and Latines, and yet we are heere shewed to disobey them,
euen in their owne numbers and quantities: taught to
produce what they make short, and make short what
690 they produce: made beleeue to be shewd measures in
that forme we haue not seene, and no such matter:
tolde that heere is the perfect Art of versifying, which
in conclusion is yet confessed to be vnperfect, as if our
Aduersary to be opposite to vs, were become vnfaith-
full to himselfe, and seeking to leade vs out of the way

of reputation, hath aduentured to intricate and confound him in his owne courses, running vpon most vn-
euen groundes, with imperfect rules, weake proofes,
and vnlawfull lawes. Whereunto the world, I am
perswaded, is not so vnreasonable as to subscribe, 700
considering the vniust authoritie of the Law-giuer.
For who hath constituted him to be the *Radaman-
thus* thus to torture sillables, and adiudge them their
perpetuall doome, setting his *Theta* or marke of con-
demnation vppon them, to indure the appoynted
sentence of his crueltie, as hee shall dispose. As
though there were that disobedience in our wordes,
as they would not be ruled or stand in order without
so many intricate Lawes, which would argue a great
peruersenesse amongst them, according to that, *in* 710
pessima republica plurimæ leges: or, that they were so
farre gone from the quiet freedome of nature, that
they must thus be brought backe againe by force.
And now in what case were this poore state of words,
if in like sorte another tyrant the next yeere should
arise and abrogate these lawes and ordaine others
cleane contrary according to his humor, and say that
they were onely right, the others vniust, what dis-
turbance were there here, to whome should we obey?
Were it not farre better to holde vs fast to our old cus- 720
tome, than to stand thus distracted with vncertaine
Lawes, wherein Right shal haue as many faces as it
pleases Passion to make it, that wheresoeuer mens
affections stand, it shall still looke that way. What
trifles doth our vnconstant curiositie cal vp to contend for, what colours are there laid vpon indifferent
things to make them seeme other then they are, as if
it were but only to intertaine contestation amongst
men; who standing according to the prospectiue of
their owne humour, seeme to see the selfe same things 730

(149)

to appeare otherwise to them, than either they doe to other, or are indeede in themselues, being but all one in nature. For what a doe haue we heere, what strange precepts of Arte about the framing of an Iambique verse in our language, which when all is done, reaches not by a foote, but falleth out to be the plaine ancient verse consisting of tenne sillables or fiue feete, which hath euer beene vsed amongest vs time out of minde. And for all this cunning and coun-
740 terfeit name can or will be any other in nature then it hath beene euer heretofore: and this new *Dimeter* is but the halfe of this verse diuided in two, and no other then the *Cæsura* or breathing place in the middest thereof, and therefore it had bene as good to haue put two lines in one, but only to make them seeme diuerse. Nay it had beene much better for the true English reading and pronouncing thereof, without violating the accent, which now our Aduersarie hath heerein most vnkindely doone: for, being, as wee are
750 to sound it, according to our English March, we must make a rest, and raise the last sillable, which falles out very vnnaturall in *Desolate*, *Funerall*, *Elizabeth*, *Prodigall*, and in all the rest sauing the Monosillables. Then followes the English *Trochaicke*, which is saide to bee a simple verse, and so indeede it is, being without Ryme; hauing here no other grace then that in sound it runnes like the knowne measure of our former ancient Verse, ending (as we terme it according to the French) in a feminine foote, sauing that it is shorter
760 by one sillable at the beginning, which is not much missed, by reason it falles full at the last. Next comes the *Elegiacke*, being the fourth kinde, and that likewise is no other then our old accustomed measure of fiue feete, if there be any difference, it must be made in the reading, and therein wee must stand bound to

stay where often we would not, and sometimes either breake the accent, or the due course of the word. And now for the other foure kinds of numbers, which are to be employed for *Odes*, they are either of the same measure, or such as haue euer beene familiarly vsed amongst vs. So that of all these eight seuerall kindes of new promised numbers you see what we haue. Onely what was our owne before, and the same but apparelled in forraine Titles, which had they come in their kinde and naturall attire of Ryme, wee should neuer haue suspected that they had affected to be other, or sought to degenerate into strange manners, which now we see was the cause why they were turnd out of their proper habite, and brought in as Aliens, onely to induce men to admire them as farre-commers. But see the power of Nature, it is not all the artificiall couerings of wit that can hide their natiue and originall condition which breakes out thorow the strongest bandes of affectation, and will be it selfe, doe Singularitie what it can. And as for those imagined quantities of sillables, which haue bin euer held free and indifferent in our language, who can inforce vs to take knowlege of them, being *in nullius verba iurati*, & owing fealty to no forraine inuention; especially in such a case where there is no necessitie in Nature, or that it imports either the matter or forme, whether it be so, or otherwise. But euery Versifier that wel obserues his worke, findes in our language, without all these vnnecessary precepts, what numbers best fitte the Nature of her Idiome, and the proper places destined to such accents, as she will not let in, to any other roomes then into those for which they were borne. As for example, you cannot make this fall into the right sound of a Verse,

None thinkes reward rendred worthy his worth:

vnlesse you thus misplace the accent vppon *Rendrèd* and *Worthìe*, contrary to the nature of these wordes: which sheweth that two feminine numbers (or Trochies, if so you wil call them) will not succeede in the third and fourth place of the Verse. And so likewise in this case,

Though Death doth consume, yet Virtue preserues,

it wil not be a Verse, though it hath the iust sillables, without the same number in the second, and the altering of the fourth place, in this sorte:

Though Death doth ruine, Virtue yet preserues.

Againe, who knowes not that we cannot kindely answere a feminine number with a masculine Ryme, or (if you will so terme it) a *Trochei* with a *Sponde*, as *Weakenes* with *Confesse*, *Nature* and *Indure*, onely for that thereby wee shall wrong the accent, the chiefe Lord and graue Gouernour of Numbers. Also you cannot in a Verse of foure feete, place a *Trochei* in the first, without the like offence, as,

Yearely out of his watry Cell:

for so you shall sound it *Yearelìè* which is vnnaturall. And other such like obseruations vsually occurre, which Nature and a iudiciall eare, of themselues teach vs readily to auoyde.

But now for whom hath our Aduersary taken all this paines? For the Learned, or for the Ignorant, or for himselfe, to shew his owne skill? If for the Learned, it was to no purpose, for euerie Grammarian in this land hath learned his *Prosodia*, and alreadie knowes all this Arte of Numbers: if for the Ignorant, it was vaine: For if they become Versifiers, wee are like to haue leane Numbers, instede of fat Ryme: and if *Tully* would haue his Orator skilld in all the knowledges appertaining to God and man, what should they haue, who would be a degree aboue Orators?

Why then it was to shew his owne skill, and what himselfe had obserued: so he might well haue done, without doing wrong to the honor of the dead, wrong to
the fame of the liuing, and wrong to *England*, in seeking to lay reproach vppon her natiue ornaments, and 840
to turne the faire streame and full course of her accents, into the shallow current of a loose vncertaintie,
cleane out of the way of her knowne delight. And I
had thought it could neuer haue proceeded from the
pen of a Scholler (who sees no profession free from the
impure mouth of the scorner) to say the reproach of
others idle tongues is the curse of Nature vpon vs,
when it is rather her curse vpon him, that knowes not
how to vse his tongue. What, doth he think himselfe
is now gotten so farre out of the way of contempt, 850
that his numbers are gone beyond the reach of oblo-
quie, and that how friuolous, or idle soeuer they shall
runne, they shall be protected from disgrace, as
though that light rymes and light numbers did not
weigh all alike in the graue opinion of the wise. And
that it is not Ryme, but our ydle Arguments that
hath brought downe to so base a reckning, the price
and estimation of writing in this kinde. When the
few good things of this age, by comming together in
one throng and presse with the many bad, are not dis- 860
cerned from them, but ouer-looked with them, and
all taken to be alike. But when after-times shall
make a quest of inquirie, to examine the best of this
Age, peraduenture there will be found in the now contemned recordes of Ryme, matter not vnfitting the
grauest Diuine, and seuerest Lawyer in this kingdome. But these things must haue the date of Antiquitie, to make them reuerend and authentical: For
euer in the collation of Writers, men rather weigh
their age then their merite, *& legunt priscos cum re-* 870

uerentia, quando coetaneos non possunt sine inuidia.
And let no writer in Ryme be any way discouraged in
his endeuour by this braue allarum, but rather ani-
mated to bring vp all the best of their powers, and
charge with all the strength of nature and industrie
vpon contempt, that the shew of their reall forces
may turne backe insolencie into her owne holde. For,
be sure that innouation neuer workes any ouerthrow,
but vpon the aduantage of a carelesse idlenesse. And
880 let this make vs looke the better to our feete, the better to our matter, better to our maners. Let the Aduersary that thought to hurt vs, bring more profit and
honor, by being against vs, then if he had stoode still
on our side. For that (next to the awe of heauen) the
best reine, the strongst hand to make men keepe their
way, is that which their enemy beares vpon them: and
let this be the benefite wee make by being oppugned,
and the meanes to redeeme backe the good opinion,
vanitie and idlenesse haue suffered to be wonne from
890 vs; which, nothing but substance and matter can effect. For,

    Scribendi rectè sapere est & principium & fons.

When we heare Musicke, we must be in our eare,
in the vtter-roome of sense, but when we intertaine
iudgement, we retire into the cabinet and innermost
withdrawing chamber of the soule: And it is but as
Musicke for the eare,

    Verba sequi fidibus modulanda Latinis,

but it is a worke of power for the soule,

900   *Numerósque modósque ediscere vitæ.*

The most iudiciall and worthy spirites of this Land
are not so delicate, or will owe so much to their eare,
as to rest vppon the out-side of wordes, and be inter-
tained with sound: seeing that both Number, Measure, and Ryme, is but as the ground or seate, where-

upon is raised the work that commends it, and which may be easily at the first found out by any shallow conceipt: as wee see some fantasticke to beginne a fashion, which afterward grauity it selfe is faine to put on, because it will not be out of the weare of other men, and *Recti apud nos locum tenet error vbi publicus factus est.* And power and strength that can plant it selfe any where, hauing built within this compasse, and reard it of so high a respect, wee now imbrace it as the fittest dwelling for our inuention, and haue thereon bestowed all the substance of our vnderstanding to furnish it as it is: and therefore heere I stand foorth, onelie to make good the place we haue thus taken vp, and to defend the sacred monuments erected therein, which containe the honour of the dead, the fame of the liuing, the glory of peace, and the best power of our speach, and wherin so many honorable spirits haue sacrificed to Memorie their dearest passions, shewing by what diuine influence they haue beene moued, and vnder what starres they liued.

But yet now notwithstanding all this which I haue heere deliuered in the defence of Ryme, I am not so farre in loue with mine owne mysterie, or will seeme so froward, as to bee against the reformation, and the better setling these measures of ours. Wherein there be many things, I could wish were more certaine and better ordered, though my selfe dare not take vpon me to be a teacher therein, hauing so much neede to learne of others. And I must confesse, that to mine owne eare, those continuall cadences of couplets vsed in long and continued Poemes, are very tyresome, and vnpleasing, by reason that still, me thinks, they runne on with a sound of one nature, and a kinde of certaintie which stuffs the delight rather then intertaines it. But yet notwithstanding, I must not out of mine owne daintinesse, condemne this kinde of writing, which peraduenture to another may seeme most delightfull, and many worthy compositions we see to haue passed with commendation in that kinde. Besides, me thinkes sometimes, to beguile the eare, with a running out, and passing ouer the Ryme, as no bound to stay vs in the line where the violence of the matter will breake thorow, is rather gracefull then otherwise. Wherein I finde my *Homer-Lucan*, as if he gloried to seeme to haue no bounds, albeit hee were confined within his measures, to be in my conceipt most happy. For so thereby, they who care not for Verse or Ryme, may passe it ouer without taking notice thereof, and please themselues with a well-measured Prose. And I must confesse my Aduersary hath wrought this much vpon me, that I thinke a Tragedie would indeede best comporte with a blank Verse, and dispence with Ryme, sauing in the *Chorus* or where a sentence shall require a couplet. And to auoyde this ouer-glutting the eare with that alwayes certaine, and ful incounter of Ryme, I haue assaid in some of my Epistles to alter the vsuall place of meeting, and to sette it further off by one Verse, to trie how I could disuse my owne eare and to ease it of this continuall burthen, which indeede seemes to surcharge it a little too much, but as yet I cannot come to please my selfe therein: this alternate or crosse Ryme holding still the best place in my affection.

Besides, to me this change of number in a Poem of one nature sits not so wel, as to mixe vncertainly, feminine Rymes with masculine, which, euer since I was warned of that deformitie by my kinde friend and countriman Maister *Hugh Samford*, I haue alwayes so auoyded it, as there are not aboue two couplettes in that kinde in all my Poem of the Ciuill warres: and

I would willingly if I coulde, haue altered it in all the rest, holding feminine Rymes to be fittest for Ditties, and either to be set certaine, or else by themselues. But in these things, I say, I dare not take vpon mee to teach that they ought to be so, in respect my selfe holdes them to be so, or that I thinke it right; for indeede there is no right in these things that are continually in a wandring motion, carried with the violence of our vncertaine likings, being but onely the time that giues them their power. For if this right, or truth, should be no other thing then that wee make it, we shall shape it into a thousand figures, seeing this excellent painter Man, can so well lay the colours which himselfe grindes in his owne affections, as that hee will make them serue for any shadow, and any counterfeit. But the greatest hinderer to our proceedings, and the reformation of our errours, is this Selfe-loue, whereunto we Versifiers are euer noted to be especially subiect; a disease of all other, the most dangerous, and incurable, being once seated in the spirits, for which there is no cure, but onely by a spirituall remedy. *Multos puto, ad sapientiam potuisse peruenire, nisi putassent se peruenisse:* and this opinion of our sufficiencie makes so great a cracke in our iudgement, as it wil hardly euer holde any thing of worth, *Cæcus amor sui*, and though it would seeme to see all without it, yet certainely it discernes but little within. For there is not the simplest writer that will euer tell himselfe, he doth ill, but as if he were the parasite onely to sooth his owne doings, perswades him that his lines can not but please others, which so much delight himselfe:

Suffenus est quisque sibi. — *neque idem vnquam.*
Æque est beatus, ac poema cum scribit,
Tam gaudet in se tamque se ipse miratur.

(157)

And the more to shew that he is so, we shall see him
euermore in all places, and to all persons repeating
his owne compositions: and,

Quem vero arripuit, tenet occiditque legendo.

Next to this deformitie stands our affectation,
wherein we alwayes bewray our selues to be both vnkinde, and vnnaturall to our owne natiue language,
in disguising or forging strange or vnvsuall wordes, as
if it were to make our verse seeme an other kind of
1020 speach out of the course of our vsuall practise, displacing our wordes, or inuesting new, onely vpon a
singularitie: when our owne accustomed phrase, set
in the due place, would expresse vs more familiarly
and to better delight, than all this idle affectation of
antiquitie, or noueltie can euer doe. And I can not
but wonder at the strange presumption of some men
that dare so audaciously aduenture to introduce any
whatsoeuer forraine wordes, be they neuer so strange;
and of themselues as it were, without a Parliament,
1030 without any consent, or allowance, establish them as
Free-denizens in our language. But this is but a Char-
acter of that perpetuall reuolution which wee see to
be in all things that neuer remaine the same, and we
must heerein be content to submit our selues to the
law of time, which in few yeeres wil make al that, for
which we now contend, *Nothing*.

FINIS.

Ulisses and the Syren

Vlisses *and the* Syren.

Syren. COme worthy Greeke, *Vlisses* come
Possesse these shores with me:
The windes and Seas are troublesome,
And heere we may be free.
   Here may we sit, and view their toile
That trauaile in the deepe,
And ioy the day in mirth the while,
And spend the night in sleepe.

   Vlis. Faire Nimph, if fame, or honor were   10
To be attaynd with ease
Then would I come, and rest me there,
And leaue such toyles as these.
   But here it dwels, and here must I
With danger seeke it forth,
To spend the time luxuriously
Becomes not men of worth.

   Syr. Vlisses, O be not deceiu'd
With that vnreall name:
This honour is a thing conceiu'd,   20
And rests on others fame.
   Begotten onely to molest
Our peace, and to beguile
(The best thing of our life) our rest,
And giue vs vp to toile.

   Vlis. Delicious Nimph, suppose there were
Nor honour, nor report,

Yet manlines would scorne to weare
The time in idle sport.
  For toyle doth giue a better touch,   30
To make vs feele our ioy;
And ease findes tediousnesse as much
As labour yeelds annoy.

  Syr. Then pleasure likewise seemes the shore,
Whereto tends all your toyle,
Which you forgo to make it more,
And perish oft the while.
  Who may disporte them diuersly,
Finde neuer tedious day,
And ease may haue varietie,   40
As well as action may.

  Vlis. But natures of the noblest frame
These toyles, and dangers please,
And they take comfort in the same,
As much as you in ease.
  And with the thought of actions past
Are recreated still;
When pleasure leaues a touch at last,
To shew that it was ill.

  Sy. That doth opinion onely cause,   50
That's out of custome bred,
Which makes vs many other lawes
Then euer Nature did.
  No widdowes waile for our delights,
Our sportes are without bloud,
The world we see by warlike wights
Receiues more hurt then good.

  Vlis. But yet the state of things require
These motions of vnrest,

And these great Spirits of high desire,   60
Seeme borne to turne them best.
   To purge the mischiefes that increase,
And all good order mar:
For oft we see a wicked peace
To be well chang'd for war.

   Sy. Well, well *Vlisses* then I see,
I shall not haue thee heere,
And therefore I will come to thee,
And take my fortunes there.
   I must be wonne that cannot win,   70
Yet lost were I not wonne:
For beauty hath created bin,
T'vndoo, or be vndonne.

FINIS.

Variant Readings

VARIANT READINGS

IN THE following pages are listed corrected misprints in the first editions (*A*) of the various items, and such variants from *A*, in the early editions and in Grosart, as actually affect the sense. Thus, the obvious misprint 'Tbat' (for 'That') in the first edition of the 'Epistle to the Countesse of Cumberland' is duly entered, but not the equally obvious 'Dut' (for 'But') in the fifth (1623) edition of *Musophilus*, line 887. Differences in spelling and punctuation pass unnoticed, except in the relatively rare cases where they affect, or came to affect, the sense. A case of this kind is the contracted spelling 'imag'ry' in the 1594 *Delia*, which was so misinterpreted that the original 'ymagery' (XLV, 9) became 'imaginary' in 1595 and 1598. Misprints corrected in contemporary *errata* lists are not recorded unless they appeared in *A*, or led to trouble afterwards. The long *s* is replaced throughout, and minor corrections in spacing and typography have been silently introduced.

As for manner of reference, the editions of each work are indicated by capital letters. A reading at the left of the bracket is that of the present edition; where a figure alone stands on that side the whole line is meant. A reading followed by a group of letters is that of all the editions indicated — the reading, but not necessarily the spelling, which need only be that of the earliest edition in the group. Where a single letter follows a reading on the right, the variant side, of the bracket, and there is no letter after the reading on the left, it is understood that the variant occurs only in the edition indicated. So in *Delia*, 1, 14, the entry 'though] thought *G*' means that 'thought' occurs in 1611 for 'though' in the six preceding editions, the later folio, Grosart, and the present text. A reading followed by a letter and a plus sign is that of the edition indicated and of subsequent editions to 1623; and similarly a reading followed by a combination like *AC–F* would be that of the first edition, and of the third, *fourth, fifth*, and sixth editions of the work in question.

No account has been taken of variations between different copies of an edition, though such variations exist and are not without interest. Thus, of the two copies of the 1602 *Works* in the Harvard College Library, one, the Brooke copy (14453.48.3), agrees with the original in giving *Rosamond*, 97, as

Ah me (poore wench) on this vnhappy shelfe.

It had been altered, however, in the 1601 issue to

Ay me (poore wench) on that vnhappy shelfe,

which is the reading of the Chew copy, 14453.48.2F. This second copy, in its turn, lacks the word 'eu'ry' in *Musophilus*, 723,

Since eu'ry change the reuerence doth decay,

although the line is correctly printed in 14453.48.3. There are several variations, affecting *Musophilus*, 792–858, between the British Museum copy C.34.a.46 and the W. A. White copy of the 1607 *Small Workes*. Mr. Sellers notes that C.34.a.46 has a cancel at this point, sig. O7. In listing the editions of each work, the copy used is given in parentheses.

TO THE READER

Editions are referred to as follows:

A   CERTAINE SMALL WORKES 1607 (*British Museum*)
B   *Ditto*   1611 (*Harvard*)
Gros.   GROSART'S ed., *I, 12–15. There are no paragraphs in B*
at lines 11, 35.

   7   the] this *B*
  10   thats] that *B*
  14   and *Gros.*] aud *A & B*
  15   minde. *Gros.*] minde *AB*
  18   will. *Gros.*] will *A* wil. *B*
  24   These] Those *Gros.*
  36   do] to *Gros.*
  42   it¹] in *A*
  46   an *A*] and *B Gros.*
  48   looks] lookt *Gros.*
  58   right.] right *A*
  66   sence. *Gros.*] sence *AB*
  67   measures] measure *B*
  78   what] that *B*
  82   touch. *Gros.*] touch *AB*
  96   els I wrote, *Ed.*] els, I wrote *A* els I wrote *B* els I wrote.
       Gros.

DELIA

Editions are referred to as follows:

New. *Sonnets after* ASTROPHEL AND STELLA (*for Thomas New-*
  man),   1591 (*British Museum*)

A DELIA *and* ROSAMOND (*50 sonnets*), 1592 (*Pforzheimer*)
B   *Ditto*   (*54 sonnets*), 1592 (*Widener*)
C DELIA AND ROSAMOND AUGMENTED, 1594 (*Widener*)
D   *Ditto*   1595 (*Huntington*)
E [*Ditto*   1598](*British Museum*)
F WORKS,   1601, 1602 (*Harvard*)
Songs *John Daniel's* SONGS (*2 sonnets*), 1606 (*British Museum*)
G CERTAINE SMALL WORKES   1611 (*Harvard*)
H WHOLE WORKES,   1623 (*Harvard*)

Gros. GROSART'S *ed., I, 33–77, recorded only as it differs from*
H. *New., an obviously corrupt, surreptitious edition, has what seem*
to be the earliest versions of the twenty-four sonnets which reappeared
in A, the first authorized edition, or B. Many revisions and some
additional poems are found in B, C, and F; while in C and F a few
sonnets are omitted, and these do not occur in subsequent editions,
except Gros.

To the Countesse of Pembroke, 19 *vnboldned B Gros.*] *vnholdned A*
  25 *Whereby B*] *Wherbey A Wherby Gros.*
  28 *lines AB*] *times Gros.*
  30 *and B Gros.*] *aud A*

To the Countesse of Pembroke AB Gros.] *om.* C–H, *but* C–E *have*
instead this sonnet, given also by Gros.:

TO THE RIGHT HONO-
RABLE, THE LADY *MARY,*
Countesse of *Pembrooke.*

WOnder of these, glory of other times,
  O thou whom Enuy eu'n is forst t'admyre:
Great Patroness of these my humble Rymes,
Which thou from out thy greatnes doost inspire:

Sith onely thou hast deign'd to rayse them higher,
  Vouchsafe now to accept them as thine owne,
  Begotten by thy hand, and my desire,
  Wherein my Zeale, and thy great might is showne.
And seeing this vnto the world is knowne,
  O leaue not, still to grace thy worke in mee: (10)
  Let not the quickning seede be ouer-throwne,
  Of that which may be borne to honour thee.
Whereof, the trauaile I may challenge mine,
  But yet the glory, (Madam) must be thine.

(7)   *thy CD Gros.*] *thine E*

I, 13   though] thought *G*
  14   Who] who *A*

II *A–H*] *appears as the first sonnet (but unnumbered) in New.,*
      where it is headed: The Author of this Poeme, S. D.
  1   infants] infant *New.*
  2   *Minerua C–EGH New.*] Minerua *AB* Minarua *F*
  3   Present] That beares *New.*
 12   pittie with your] crueltie with *New.*
 13   that *A Gros.*] her *B–H New.:*   you *A–D Gros.*] ye *E–*
     H: beg till you haue moou'd] say, I perish for *New.*
 14] And feare this deed wil make the world abhor her.   *New.*

III *A–H*] *appears as Sonnet 1 in New.*
  1   this] the *New.*
  2   sad and mornefull *A–E Gros.*] lamentable *F–H* and af-
     flicted *New.*
  3   afflicted are] to mee doo fare *New.*
  4   Let them yet sigh their owne *AB Gros.*] Ah let them
     sigh theyr owne *C–E* Let them sigh for their owne *F–H*
     May moue them sigh thereat *New.*
  6   so great distresse *A–E Gros.*] my heauines *F–H* my soules
     distresse *New.*
  7   soone] will *New.*
  8   ones *A–E Gros.*] soules *F–H*
  8] Whilst blind ones see no error in my verse. *New.*
  9   youth and errours lead *A–E*] youth & errour leade *F–H*
     hap and error leades *New.*
 10   your] the *New.*
 11   Ah *A–E Gros. New.*] Do *F–H:*   sorrowes read] sor-
     row reads *New.*
 12   wrongs] wrong *New.*

IIII, 8   how *AB Gros.*] where *C–H:*   hath *A–D*] haue *E+*
11   craue *AB*] beare *C+*
12   *AB*] Of intercession to a Tyrants will. *C–E*
     Of intercession, but to moue her will. *F–H*

V,   4   *Diana*-like *C+*] Diana-like *AB*
5   my view *AB*] mine eye *C–G* mine eyes *H*
7   sweet] most (*corrected in Errata*) *A*
8   Castes *A–E*] Cast *F+*
10   whilst *ABG*] while *C–FH*

VI, 2   brow shades *A–D Gros.*] browshades *E–G* brow-shades *H*
13   O *A–E*] For *F+*

VII, 1   O *A–D*] For *F–H*
8   had *A–DFG*] have *H*
13   not I *AB*] I not *CDF–H*

VIII, 2   incens *B–DF–H*] incens *A*
13   her *A–D*] *om. F–H*
14   leaue *A Gros.*] cease *B–DF–H:*   her *A–D*] *om. F–H*

IX *A–DF–H*] *appears as Sonnet 22 in New.*
1   to *A–DH New.*] *om. F om.* (*corrected in Errata*) *G*
2   Painte *A–DF–H*] To paint *New. Gros.:*   shore, *A*] shore
     B–DF–H New.]
3   downward lookes, still reading *A–DF–H*] prone aspect
     still treading *New.*
4   The *A–DFG*] These *H:*   loues *A–DFH*] loue *G*
4   *A–DF–H*] Sad horror, pale griefe, prostrate dispaire:
     New.
6   Lye downe to waile, rise vp *B–DF–H*] Lye downe to
     waile, rise vp *A* Rise vp to waile, lie downe *New.:*   and
     A–DF–H] to *New.:*   me *AB New.*] *om. CDF–H*
7   *A–DF–H*]
     With ceaseles toyle Cares restlesse stones to roule, *New.*
8   my greifes *A–DF–H*] and mone *New.:*   and *AB*]
     whilst *CDF–H New.:*   me *AB New.*] *om. CDF–H*
12   my¹ *A*] mine *B–DF–H*
9–12   *A–DF–H*] If this be Loue, to languish in such care,
     Loathing the light, the world, my selfe, and all,
     With interrupted sleepes fresh griefes repaire,
     And breath out horror in perplexed thrall: *New.*
14   O then loue I *A–D*] Then do I loue *F–H* Loe then loue I
     New.

X, 1 O then I loue *A*] O then loue I *B–D* Then do I loue *F–H*
4 wrought *A–D*] wrote *F–H*
5 O thou *A–D*] Thou powre *F–H*
6 Goddesse *B–DF–H*] Gods *A*
14 me. *B–DF–H*] me, *A*

XI *A–DF–H*] *appears as Sonnet 4 in New.*
1 win *A–DF–H*] gaines *New.*:   hart *A–DF–H*] hearts
New.
9 *A–DF–H*] Though frozen will may not be thawed with
teares, *New.*
11 be to so deafe *A–DF–H*] be made to deafned *New.*
12 though *A–DF–H*] though, *New. Gros.*

XII,1 white *AB*] purest *CDF–H*:   wings, *CDF–H*] wings: *A*
winges, *B*
6 mee *AB*] *om. CDF–H*
8 mee *AB*] *om. CDF–H*
11 wheele, *A*] wheele's *B–DFG* wheeles *H*

XIII *A–H*] *appears as Sonnet 7 (misprinted 71) in New.*
2 proper griefe] griefe himselfe *New.*
6 my *AB New.*] mine *C–H*:   harte, *Ed.*] harte: *AB* hart,
C–H hart *New.*
7 fayrest forme] goodliest shape *New.*:   the worldes eye
AB] that all the world *C–H* that the worlds eye *New.*
(*cf.* XV, 13)
10 sweetest grace I doe] sweete *Idea* I *New.*
13 O *A–E New.*] But *F–H*:   happie] blessed *New.*:
ioy'd] ioyes *New.*

XIIII *A–H*] *appears as Sonnet 6 in New.*
1 Those¹] These *New.*:   amber *AB New.*] snary *C–H*
4 darte] darts *New.*:   those] these *New.*
6 wounde] stroke *New.*:   do *A–E*] can *F–H New.*
8 this] that *New.*
9 and] I *New.*
10 The . . . the . . . the] This . . . this . . . this *New.*
13 Yet] Yer (*corrected in Errata*) *A*
14 *Delia*] Ladie *New.*

XV *A–H*] *appears as Sonnet 14 in New.*
1 that a loyall] a true *New.*
5 caracters *New.*] caracterss *A* characters *B–FH* charec-
ters *G*

(173)

6 spoken, *C New.*] spoken; *AB* spoken *D–H*
7 that] which *New.*
9–12] If I haue wept the day, and sigthd [*sic*] the night,
   Whilst thrice the Sun approcht this northern bound:
   If such a faith hath euer wrought aright,
   And well deserud, and yet no fauour found: *New.*
13 the world yet *AB*] that all the world *C–H* the
   wholeworld it *New.* (*cf.* XIII, 7)
14 hurt must] most hurt *New.*

XVI *A–H*] *appears as Sonnet 19 in New.*
3 *AB New.*] My ioyes but shadowes, touch of truth my
   anguish, *C–H*
4 hurt, inur'd *AB*] heart mooued *New.*
4] Griefes euer springing, comforts neuer borne. *C–H*
5 *AB New.*] And still expecting when she will relent, *C–H*
6 Hoarce *AB New.*] Growne hoarce *C–H:* yet my
   merit *AB New.*] gyue *C–H*
7 euer made I *AB New.*] hauing spent *C–H*
8 *AB New.*] That weary of my selfe, I loathe to lyue. *C–E*
   life [*for* selfe *C–E*] *F–H*
9 But still *AB*] And yet *C–H* Yet since *New.:*   renuing,
   AB] renewes, *CD* renues *E–H* renewing, *New.*
10 Reuiues new *AB*] Still new-borne *C–H* Reuiues still
   New.:   disdayning *AB New.*] disdaine *C–H*
11 Still must I goe *AB New.*] And still my hope *C–H:*
   pursuing *AB New.*] pursues *C–H*
12 payning *AB*] paine *C–H*
12] And nothing but hir loue and my harts paining. *New.*
13 Waile all my life *AB*] This is my state *C–H:*   do *A–FH*]
   did *G*
13] Weep howrs, grieue daies, sigh months, & still mourn
   yearly, *New.*
14 And thus I liue *B–H*] And this I liue *A* Thus must I doe
   New.

XVI] *after this sonnet C–H have:*

WHy should I sing in verse, why should I frame,
   These sad neglected notes for her deere sake?
Why should I offer vp vnto her name,
   The sweetest sacrifice my youth can make?
Why should I striue to make her liue for euer,
   That neuer deignes to giue me ioy to liue?

(174)

Why should m'afflicted Muse so much endeuour,
　Such honour vnto crueltie to giue?
If her defects haue purchast her this fame,
　What should her vertues doe, her smiles, her loue?　(10)
　If this her worst, how should her best inflame?
　What passions would her milder fauours moue?
Fauours (I thinke) would sence quite ouer-come,
And that makes happy Louers euer dombe.

(9)　If *C–G Gros.*] I *H*

XVII *AB*] *appears as Sonnet 15 in New.* XVIII *C–H*
　3　terror *ABF–H New.*] error (*corrected in Errata*) *C* error
　　　DE
　5　leaue] haue *New.*
　6　exact] exacts *New.*
　8　true and loyall loue] long and pure a faith *New.*:
　　　fauours *A*] fauour *B–H New.*

XVIII *AB*] *appears as Sonnet 11 in New.* XIX *CDF–H*
　1　tresses *A–DF–H*] treasure *New.*
　6　odors *A–DF–H*] odor *New.*
　9　thy *A–DF–H*] the *New.*:　　　　resign'd *B–DF–H New.*]
　　　resigned *A*
　10　giue backe vnto the *A–DF–H*] yeeld to *Hermonius New.*

XVIII] *after this sonnet F–H have:*

　　W Hat it is to breathe and liue without life:
　　　　How to be pale with anguish, red with feare:
　T'haue peace abroad, and nought within but strife:
　Wish to be present, and yet shun t'appeare:
How to be bold far off, and bashfull neare:
　　How to think much, and haue no words to speake:
　To craue redresse, yet hold affliction deare:
　To haue affection strong, a bodie weake:
Neuer to finde, and euermore to seeke:
　　And seeke that which I dare not hope to finde:　(10)
　T'affect this life, and yet this life disleeke:
　Gratefull t'another, to my selfe vnkinde.
This cruell knowledge of these contraries,
Delia my hart hath learnd out of those eies.

(1)　without *GH*] wirhout *F*
(2)　feare: *Ed.*] feare· *F* feare. *G* feare *H* feare, *Gros.*

(175)

XIX *AB*] *appears as Sonnet 20 in New.* XX *CD* XXI *F–H*

1   thus be clouded *A–DF–H*] bright be doubled *New.*

2   shines no comfort *A–DF–H*] cannot shine through *New.*

3   *A–DF–H*] And Disdaines vapors are thus ouergrowen, *New.*

4   thus wholy darkned *A–D*] wholy in–darkned *F–H* to me quite darkened *New.*

5   *A–DF–H*] Why trouble I the world then with my cries, *New.*

7   Since *AB New.*] Sith *CDF–H:* ruthlesse *A–DF–H*] ruthfull *New.*

8   vntun'd *A–DF–H*] my vntuned *New.*

11   must holde her *A–DF–H*] hold her most *New.:* till after *A–DF–H*] vntill my *New.*

12   a *A–D*] one *New.*

12]   And that all this mooues not her thoughts a whit, *F–H*

13–14   *A–D New.*] Yet sure she cannot but must thinke a part, She doth me wrong, to grieue so true a hart. *F–H*

XX *AB*] *appears as Sonnet 21 (misprinted 2) in New.* XXI *C–E* XXII *F–H*

2   appealeth *AB New.*] appeales *C–E*

4   desiers *B*] desires (*corrected in Errata*) *A*

4]   Whilst age vpon my wasted body steales. *C–E* Whiles dearest blood my fierie passions sealeth. *New.*

5   is now *AB New.*] being made *C–E*

6   lyueth *AB New.*] liues *C–E*

7   sees *A–D*] seest *E* knowes *New.*

8   Yet *A–E*] And *New.:* giueth *AB New.*] giues *C–E*

9   *B–E New.*] *not indented in A:* her[1] *A–E*] the *New.*

12   liues *A–E*] soules *New.*

13   That *AB New.*] Which *C–E*

14   So *A–E*] Thus *New.:* disgraces fall. *B–E*] disgraces fall, *A* disgrace do fall. *New.*

XX]   *F–H have this version:*

COme Tyme the anchor-hold of my desire,
  My last Resort whereto my hopes appeale,
Cause once the date of her disdaine t'expire:
Make her the sentence of her wrath repeale.
Rob her faire Brow, breake in on Beautie, steale
Powre from those eyes, which pittie cannot spare:

Deale with those daintie cheekes as she doth deale
With this poore heart consumed with dispaire.
This heart made now the prospectiue of care,
  By louing her, the cruelst Faire that liues   (10)
  The cruelst Fayre that sees I pine for her,
  And neuer mercie to my merit giues.
Let her not still triumph ouer the prize
Of mine affections taken by her eies.

  (6)   those *FH*] these *G*
(12)   my *FG*] thy *H*

XX] *after this sonnet F–H have the following, which appears also
in* John Daniel's Songs, *1606:*

TYme, cruell tyme, come and subdue that Brow
  Which conquers all but thee, and thee too staies
As if she were exempt from Syeth or Bow,
From loue or yeares vnsubiect to decaies.
Or art thou growne in league with those faire eies
  That they may helpe thee to consume our daies?
  Or dost thou spare her for her cruelties,
  Being merciles like thee that no man weies?
And yet thou seest thy powre she disobaies,
  Cares not for thee, but lets thee waste in vaine,   (10)
  And prodigall of howers and yeares betraies
Beautie and youth t'opinion and disdaine.
Yet spare her Tyme, let her exempted bee,
She may become more kinde to thee or mee.

  (1)   come and *F–H*] canst thou *Songs*
  (2)   Which *F–H*] That *Songs*
  (4)   or *F–H*] and *Songs*
  (6)   may *F–H*] might *Songs*
  (7)   spare *F–H*] loue *Songs*
(9*ff.*) *F–H*] *these lines are replaced by the following in* Songs:
      Then doe so still although shee makes no steeme,
    Of dayes nor yeares, but lets them run in vaine:
    Hould still thy swift wing'd hours that wondring seeme
    To gase on her, euen to turne back againe.
      And doe so still although she nothing cares,
    Doe as I doe, loue her although vnkinde,
    Hould still, yet O I feare at vnawares,
    Thou wilt beguile her though thou seem'st so kinde.

XXI *AB*] *appears as Sonnet 2 in New.* XXII *C–E* XXIIII *F–H*
1 smoakes *B–E*] smaokes *A* smoake *F–H* smokes *New.*
2 flame] fire *New.*
3 Are these due *AB*] Are those due *C–FH* And those due *G*
   These are the *New.*
4 vnkindnes *B–H*] vndindnes *A*
4] And these my tyrants cruell minde fulfills. *New.*
6 and she respects not it] that yet respects no whit *New.*
7 flowre vntimely's] youth, vntimely *New.*
8 And] By *New.*
10 ease *A–E New. Gros.*] case *F–H*
11 that] the *New.:*   the] that *G*
13 so] to *New.*
14 eye me *A–E New.*] els looke *F–H* els eye me *Gros.*

XXII *AB*] XXIII *CD* XXV *F–H*
2 Traytrous *A*] Traytours *B* Traytour *CDF–H*

XXIII *AB*] *appears as Sonnet 18 in New.* XXIIII *CD* XXVI
   F–H
2 care to care that leades *A–DF–H*] thought to thought
   that lead *New.*
3 *A–DF–H*] Fortunes Orphan, hers and the worlds scorne,
   New.
4 sad *A–DF–H*] bad *New.*
5 sleepe *B–DF–H New.*] sleeepe *A*
6 no sunne euer *A–DF–H*] neuer sunne yet *New.*
7 *A–D*] Th'impression of her eyes do pearce so deepe,
   F–H A pleasing griefe impressed hath so deepe, *New.*
9 But since *ABF–H*] But sith *CD* Yet since *New.:*   doth
   yeeld thus much *A–D New.*] yeelds frute so sowre *F–H*
10 may *A–DF–H*] must *New.*
11 for that the cause is such *A–D*] the cause being of this
   powre *F–H* because the cause is such *New.*
12 Ile *A–DF–H*] I *New.*
13 that wee *A–D New.*] we both *F–H*

XXIIII *AB*] *appears as Sonnet 8 in New.* XXVII *Gros. om.*
   CDF–H
1 rebel *AB Gros.*] rebels *New.*
3 shut those waies *AB Gros.*] close the way *New.*
4 Hoping *AB Gros.*] Striuing *New.*
5 *AB Gros.*] Whilest garding thus the windowes of my
   thought, *New.*

7   doe *AB Gros.*] to *New.*
10–11 *AB Gros.*] My freedomes-tyrant glorying in hir art:
       But (ah) sweete foe, small is the victorie *New.*
12   three *AB New.*] thee *Gros.*

XXV *A–E*] *appears as Sonnet 9 in New.* XXVII *F–H* XXVIII
     Gros.
   2   harts] heart *G*
   3   hard] sad *G*
   4   poore] whole *New.*
   7   Trophies] triumphs *New.*:   fall,] fall. *A*
   8   yeelde] yeelds *New.*:   that giues them their] who gaines
       them there *New.*
   9   I²] and *New.*
   12 heauie] cruell *New.*
   14 all three] them all *New.*

XXVI *A–E*] *appears as Sonnet 17 in New.* XXVIII *F–H* XXXI
     Gros.

XXVI *C–H have this heading: Alluding to the Sparrow pursued*
     by a Hauke, that flew into the bosome of Zenocrates.
   1   her *A–E New.*] thy *F–H:*   it *A–E New.*] *om. F–H*
   2   bosome of my deerest *A–E New.*] Refuge of thy brest
       F–H
   3   She there in that sweete *A–E New.*] Thy rigor in that
       F–H: it, *A–E New.*] *om. F–H*
   4   Where it presum'd *A–E*] When it had hop'd *New.*
   4] That which thy succring mercy should haue blest. *F–H*
       my [*for* thy *FH*] *G*
   5   *A–E*] No priuiledge of faith could it protect, *F–H*
       My faith of priuiledge could no whit protect it, *New.*
   6   That was *A–E New.*] Faith being *F–H:*   three *A–E*
       New.] fiue *F–H*
   7   *A–E*] Wherein no shew gaue cause of least suspect, *F–H*
       Whereby she had no cause once to suspect it: *New.*
   8   she sawe *A–E New.*] thou saw'st *F–H*
   9   And yet no comfort would her *A–E*] Yet no mild com-
       fort would thy *F–H* Yet no hopes letter would her *New.*:
       reueale mee, *New.*] reueale mee. *A* reueale me, *B–E*
       reueale, *F–H*
   10 lightning looke *A–E*] lightning lookes *F–H* comforts hue
       New.:   hopes erecteth *A–E*] hopes erect *F–H* spirits
       erecteth *New.*

(179)

11 mee *A–E New.*] om. *F–H*
12 respecteth *A–E New.*] respect *F–H*
13 where hop'd I to haue liuen *A–E*] frō whence my life should come *F–H* where I had hope to liuen *New.*
14 that hand, which *A–E*] that hand whom *F–H* her hand that *New.:*   better might haue giuen *A–E New.*] such deeds ill become *F–H*

XXVI] *after this sonnet B has:*

(i)

Still in the trace of my tormented thought,
My ceaselesse cares must martch on to my death:
Thy least regarde too deerely haue I bought,
Who to my comfort neuer deign'st a breath.
    Why should'st thou stop thine eares now to my cryes,
Whose eyes were open ready to oppresse me?
Why shutt'st thou not the cause whence all did rise,
Or heare me now, and seeke how to redresse me.
    Iniurious *Delia*, yet Ile loue thee still,
Whilst that I breath in sorrow of my smart: 10
Ile tell the world that I deseru'd but ill,
And blame my selfe for to excuse thy hart.
    Then iudge who sinnes the greater of vs twaine:
    I in my loue, or thou in thy disdaine.

(ii)

Oft doe I muse, whether my *Delias* eyes
Are eyes, or els two faire bright starres that shine:
For how could nature euer thus deuise,
Of earth on earth a substance so diuine.
    Starres sure they are, whose motions rule desires,
And calme and Tempest followe their aspects:
Their sweet appearing still such powre inspires,
That makes the world admire so strange effects.
    Yet whether fixt or wandring starres are they,
Whose influence rule the Orbe of my poore hart: 10
Fixt sure they are, but wandring make me stray,
In endles errors whence I cannot part.
    Starres then, not eyes, moue yet with milder view,
    Your sweet aspect on him that honours yow.

TO *M. P.*

Like as the spotlesse *Ermelin* distrest,
Circumpass'd round with filth and lothsome mud:
Pines in her griefe, imprisoned in her nest,
And cannot issue forth to seeke her good.

So I inuiron'd with a hatefull want,
Looke to the heauens, the heauens yeelde forth no grace,
I search the earth, the earth I finde as skant,
I view my selfe, my selfe in wofull case.

Heauen nor earth will not, my selfe cannot worke
A way through want to free my soule from care: 10
But I must pine, and in my pining lurke,
Least my sad lookes bewray me how I fare.

My fortune mantled with a clowde s'obscure,
Thus shades my life so long as wants endure.

(iv)

My cares draw on mine euerlasting night,
In horrors sable clowdes sets my liues sunne:
My liues sweet sunne, my deerest comforts light,
Will rise no more to me, whose day is dunne.

I goe before vnto the Mirtle shades,
To attend the presence of my worlds Deere:
And there prepare her flowres that neuer fades,
And all things fit against her comming there.

If any aske me why so soone I came,
Ile hide her sinne, and say it was my lot,   10
In life and death Ile tender her good name,
My life nor death shall neuer be her blot.

Although this world may seeme her deede to blame:
Th'*Elisean* ghosts shall neuer know the same.

(i)] *appears also as* XXVII *in* C–E XXIX *F–H* XXXIII *Gros.*
  1 my tormented *B–E*] one perplexed *F–H*
  2 must martch on to my death *B–E*] continually run on *F–H*
3–8 *B–E*]

> Seeking in vaine what I haue euer sought,
> One in my loue, and her hard hart still one.
> I who did neuer ioy in other Sun,
>   And haue no stars but those, that must fulfill
>   The worke of rigor, fatally begun
>   Vpon this hart, whom crueltie will kill. *F–H*

9 Ile *B–E*⌉ I *F–H*
10 *B–E*⌉ And will whilst I shall draw this breath of mine, *F–H*
12 for to excuse thy hart *B–E*⌉ t'excuse that hart of thine *F–H*
13 Then iudge *B–E*⌉ See then *F–H*

(ii)⌉ *appears also as* XXVIII *in C–E* XXX *F–H* XXXIIII *Gros.*
  1 muse, whether my *B*⌉meruaile, whether *C–H*
  2 faire bright *B*⌉ radiant *C–H*
  13 yet *B*⌉ you *C–H:* milder *B–G*⌉ a milder *H*

(iii)⌉ *appears also as* XXIX *in Gros.* (XXIX *is misprinted*
  XXXI *in B*) *om. C–H*
  9 worke *B*⌉ woke *Gros.*

(iv)⌉ *appears as Sonnet 23 in New.* XXX *Gros. om. C–H*
  1 draw on mine *B Gros.*⌉ drawes on my *New.*
  2 In *B Gros.*⌉ And *New.:* sets *B Gros.*⌉ dims *New.*
  3 *B Gros.*⌉ That my liues sunne, and thou my worldly light, *New.*
  4 Will *B Gros.*⌉ Shall *New.:* whose day is *B Gros.*⌉ my daies are *New.*
  5 I *B Gros.*⌉ Ile *New.*
  7 there prepare her *B Gros.*⌉ dresse a bed of *New.*
  9 me why *B Gros.*⌉ why that *New.*
  10 sinne *B Gros.*⌉ fault *New.*
  12 nor *B Gros.*⌉ and *New.*
  13 *B Gros.*⌉ Although the world this deed of hirs may blame, *New.*

XXVII *A*⌉ *appears as Sonnet 24 in New.* XXXI *BF–H* XXIX
    C–E XXXII *Gros.*
  1 this⌉ my *New.:* payning *AB New.*⌉ paine *C–H*
  2 wayling *A–E*⌉ griefe *F–H* crying *New.*
  3 That neuer found my fortune *AB New.*⌉ That euer found
    my fortune *C–E* Finding my fortune euer *F–H:* but
    in wayning *AB New.*⌉ in the wayne *C–H*
  4 cares my present woes assayling *A–E*⌉ cares, supplide
    with no reliefe *F–H* cares my bloud and bodie trying
    New.
  5 her *A–E New.*⌉ thee *F–H:* she might haue blest mee
    AB New.⌉ for her tis done *C–E* for thee tis done *F–H*
  6 *A–E New.*⌉ But these weake whings presuming to as-
    pire, *F–H* wings [*for* whings *FH*] G (*Gros. retains*
    whings *as a Somerset spelling*)
  7 *AB New.*⌉ Which now are melted by that glorious Sunne,
    C–E Which now are melted by thine eies bright sun, *F–H*
  8 Downe doe I *AB New.*⌉ That makes me *C–H:* desir-
    ing *A–E New.*⌉ desire *F–H*
  9 doe *AB New.*⌉ I *C–H:* mercy speedy *AB New.*⌉ helpe
    with speed *C–H*
  10 pittying⌉ piteous *New.:* mourning *A–E New.*⌉ feares
    F–H

(182)

11 *AB New.*] No succour finde I now when most I need, *C–H*
12 *A–E*] My heats must drowne in th'Oceā of my teares.
    F–H
    My Ocean teares drowne me, and quench my burning,
    New.
13 And this my death *AB New.*] Whilst my distress *C–E:*
    shall *A–E*] must *New.*
13] Which still must beare the title of my wrong, *F–H*
14 cruell Faire her *AB*] *Cruell Fayre* this *C–E*
14] Caus'd by those cruell beames that were so strong. *F–H*
    Whiles faith doth bid my cruell Faire adieu. *New.*

XXVII] *after this sonnet C–E have as* XXX, *F–H as* XXXII,
      Gros. as XXXV:

  AND yet I cannot reprehend the flight,
      Or blame th'attempt presuming so to sore,
  The mounting venter for a high delight,
  Did make the honour of the fall the more.
  For who gets wealth that puts not from the shore?
      Daunger hath honour, great designes their fame,
      Glorie doth follow, courage goes before.
      And though th'euent oft aunswers not the same,
  Suffise that high attempts haue neuer shame.
      The Meane-obseruer, (whom base Safety keepes,)   (10)
      Liues without honour, dies without a name,
      And in eternall darknes euer sleepes.
  And therefore DELIA, tis to me no blot,
      To haue attempted, though attain'd thee not.

  (7) follow, *D–H*] follow *C*
  (10) Meane-obseruer *C*] meane obseruer *D–H*

XXVIII *A*] *appears as Sonnet 27 in New.* [X]XXII *B* XXXI
      C–E XXXIII *F–H* XXXVI *Gros.*
    1 hopes] hope *New.*
    3 meanes presum'd] meane presumes *New.*
    4 Her thunder of disdaine forst] For disdaines thunderbolt
       made *New.:*   retire *A–E New. Gros.*] to retire *F–H*
    8 pride brook'd] state brooks *New.:*   come so nye her *A–
       E New.*] so aspire *F–H*
    9 aspyring *A–E New.*] desiring *F–H*

XXVIII] *it is followed in New. by the words:* Finis, Daniel.

XXIX A] *appears as Sonnet 5 in New.* XXXIII *B* XXXII *C–E*
XXXIIII *F–H* XXXVII *Gros.*

1   O why dooth *Delia A–E*] Why doost thou DELIA *F–H*
    Why doth my Mistres *New.:*   her *A–E New.*] thy *F–H*

2   her . . . her *A–E New.*] thy . . . thee *F–H*

3   dooth *A–E New.*] doest *F–H*

6   mercy-wanting *B–FH New.*] mercy wanting *A* mercie
    (wanting *G*

7   your *A–E New.*] thy *F–H*

8   you best may *A–E New.*] thou best maist *F–H*

9   your . . . your *A–E New.*] thy . . . thy *F–H*

10 what powre is in] the power of *New.:*   your *A–E New.*]
    thy *F–H*

11 viewe] admire *New.*

12 t'a] to *New.*

13] I feare your change not flower nor *Hiacynth, New.*

14 I feare your eye hath turn'd] *Medusas* eye may turne
    New.

XXX *A*] *appears as Sonnet 26 in New.* XXXIIII *B* XXXIII
    C–E XXXV *F–H* XXXVIII *Gros.*

1   see] I see *New.:*   shall] may *New.*

2   When] And *New.:*   shall] may *New.*

4   working] power *New.*

5   Then] Her *New.*

6   world dooth so] worlds eie doth *New.*

7   vp all] her praise *New.*

8   fade those flowres] fades the flower *New.:*   which deckt
    AB] that deckt *C–H* which fed *New.*

9   her² *ABF–H New.*] the *C–E*

12 shall] may *New.*

14 shall] to *New.*

XXXI *A*] XXXV *B* XXXIIII *C–E* XXXVI *F–H* XXXIX
    Gros.

1   wee steeme *AB*] we steeme *C–E* w'esteem *F–H*

3   in *A–E*] yet *F+:*   greene she doth inclose *A–E*] bud
    doth vndisclose *F+*

4   That *AF–H*] The *B–E:*   pure sweete *A–E*] full of *F+*

6   ful-blowne pride is in declyning *A–E*] wide blowne pomp
    comes to decline *F+*

8   *A–E*] So fade the Roses of those cheeks of thine. *F+*

10 blooming *A–E*] springing *F+:*   thy *A–G Gros.*] the *H*

(184)

11 Time *A–EH*] Tyme *F* ryme *G*
13 O let not then such riches *A–E*] Then do not thou such
    treasure *F*+
14 whilst that *A–E*] now whilst *F*+

XXXII *A*] XXXVI *B* XXXV *C–E* XXXVII *F–H* XL *Gros*.
4   thy *A–D*] the *E*+
10 showest *A–E*] show'st *F*+
12 hide it most, and couer lowest *A–E*] most inuaile &
    shadow most *F*+
14 they] thy *B*

XXXIII *A*] XXXVII *B* XXXVI *C–E* XXXVIII (*misprinted*
    XXXIII *F*) *F–H* XLI *Gros*.
4   thee *A*] the *B*+
8   art] are *Gros*.
11 shalt] shall *H*
14 golden *A–E*] sable *F*+

XXXIIII *A*] XXXVIII *B* XXXVII *C–E* XXXVIIII *F–H*
    XLII *Gros*.
1   golden *A–E*] sable *F*+
2   flowers *A–E*] beauties *F*+
8   thee.] thee, *A*

XXXV *A*] XXXIX *B* XXXVIII *C–E* XL *F–H* XLIII *Gros*.
5   in *A*] within *B*+
13 But *A*] For *B*+

XXXVI *A*] XL *B* XXXIX *C–E* XLI *F–H* XLIIII *Gros*.
1   O be not grieu'd *A–E*] Be not displead *FH* Be not dis-
    pleas'd *G Gros*.
3   could, *AB*] could. *C*+
4   The . . . hart. *A*] The . . . hart, *B* (The . . . hart.) *CD*
    (The . . . hart) *E–H*
7   liue,] liues *A*
8   yce] yee (*corrected in Errata*) *A*

XXXVII *Ed.*] XXVII (*misprint*) *A* XLI *B* XL *C–E* XLII *F–H*
    XLV *Gros*.
2   the which *A–E*] which proud *F*+
4   Within] within *A*
5   for all that no *A*] found I that no *B–E* neuer found that
    F–H
8   Annals] Anualls *A*

(185)

9   *A–E*] And therefore grieue not if thy beauties die, *F*+

10   her *A–E*] thee *F*+

11   mortallitie did couer *A–E*] couered mortalitie *F*+

12   Which shall *A*] Which must *B–E* And must *F–H:*   the needle *A–E*] the Needle, *FH* thee Needle, *G:*   trayle. *A*] Rayle, *B* Raile. *C–H*

13   t'in-woman *B–E*] t'in woman *A*

13] That Grace which doth more then in woman thee, *F–H*

14   her *AC*] thee *BDE*

14] Liues in my lines, and must eternall bee. *F–H*

XXXVIII *A*] XLII *B* XLI *C–E* XLIII *F–H* XLVI *Gros.*

  1   Faire *A–E*] Most faire *F*+

  3   fore-spent *A*] quite spent *B*+

  4   hopes *A–E*] hope *F*+

  5   wafte *AB*] waft *C–G Gros.* wast *H*

11   Ile not reuenge *AB*] I shall forget *C*+:   wrath *AB*] griefes *C*+

12   For *AB*] And *C*+

13   Once let the Ocean *ABF–H*] O then let th'Ocean *C–E:* cares *ABH*] care *C–G*

XXXIX *A*] XLIII *B* XLII *C–E* XLIIII *F–H* XLVII *Gros.*

  3   printed *A–E*] painted *F*+

  9] *not indented in A*

XL *A*] *appears as Sonnet 13 in New.* XLIIII *B* XLIII *C–E* XLV *F–H* XLVIII *Gros.*

  1   *Cynthia AB New.*] Delia *C–H*

  2   attending *A–E New.*] t'attend *F–H*

  3   fall] falls *New.:*   nor euer dryes *AB*] but euer rise *C–E Gros.* but euer dries *F–H* nor euer dies *New.*

  4   ending *A–E New.*] end *F–H*

  5   did] doth *New.*

  6   Soueraignes course, the nights pale] soueraigne, the night wandring *New.*

  7   paide the impost of his waues] euer hath his impost paid *New.*

  8   to her in truth haue euer *AB*] vnto her Deitie haue *CD* vnto her Deitie hath *E* vnto her crueltie hath *F–H* to my soules Queene hath *New.*

  9] Yet her hard rocke firme fixt for ay remouing, *New.*

10 these *A–G Gros.*] their *H:* with *A–CH*] c̄w *D* t̄w *E*
which *FG:* driueth *A–E*] driues *F–H*

10] No comfort to my cares she euer giueth; *New.*

11 And yet] Yet had *New.:* I] I'd *Gros.:* in *A–E New.*]
for *F–H:* loue] louing *New.*

12 I would ioy] to imbrace *New.:* liueth *A–E New.*] liues
F–H

13 I doubt to *A–E*] And if I *F–H* I feare to *New.:* in my
gayning *AC–E*] in my gaying *B* to complaine *F–H* in my
raigning *New.*

14 *A–E New.*] What should I do then if I should obtaine?
F–H

XLI *A*] XLV *B* XLIIII *C–E* XLVI *F–H* XLIX *Gros.*
   5 troubled] *om. (corrected in Errata) A*
13–14 *A–E*] I know her hart cannot but iudge with mee,
      Although her eyes my aduersaries bee. *F+*

XLII *A*] XLVI *B* XLV *C–E* XLVII *F–H* L *Gros.*
   11 *A–E*] And that in Beauties lease expir'd, appeares *F+*
   12 Dated in *A–E*] The date of *F+*
   13 hath beene often tolde *A–E*] must not be fore-told *F+*
   14 And *A–E*] For *F+*

XLIII *A*] XLVII *B* XLVI *C–E* XLVIII *F–H* LI *Gros.*
   3 a *A–G Gros.*] *om. H*
   5 Ah *A–E Gros.*] And *F–H*
   7 blossoms *AC–E*] blossomes *BH* blossome *FG*
   12 shall yeeld thee lasting *A–E*] must onely yeeld thee *F+*
   13 I hope *A–E*] Make me *F+*

XLIII] *after this sonnet C–E have as* XLVII, *F–H as* XLVIIII,
   Gros. as LII:

   At the Authors going into Italie.

O Whether (poore forsaken) wilt thou goe,
   To goe from sorrow, and thine owne distresse,
When euery place presents like face of woe,
And no remoue can make thy sorrowes lesse?
Yet goe (forsaken,) leaue these woods, these playnes,
   Leaue her and all, and all for her that leaues
Thee and thy loue forlorne, and both disdaines;
And of both, wrongfull deemes, and ill conceaues.

(187)

Seeke out some place, and see if any place
  Can giue the least release vnto thy griefe: (10)
  Conuay thee from the thought of thy disgrace,
  Steale from thy selfe, and be thy cares own thiefe.
But yet what comfort shall I heereby gaine?
Bearing the wound, I needs must feele the paine.

At the Authors going into Italie. C–E Gros.] *om. F–H*
  (1) O *C–E*] And *F–H*
 (13) comfort *C–G*] comforts *H*
 (14) wound *D–H*] wonnd *C*

XLIIII *A*] XLVIII *B–E* L *F–H* LIII *Gros.*

XLIIII] *C–E Gros. have the heading: This Sonnet was made at*
    the Authors (C misprints Authorr) beeing in Italie.
  2 turnes] tunres (*corrected in Errata*) *A*
  5 where *A–G Gros.*] were *H*
  6 smyleth *A*] now smileth *B* doth smile *C–H*
  7 beautie *AB*] eyes haue *C+*
  8 volume which her fame compyleth *AB*] wonder of our
    happy Ile *C+*
 10 *Neptunes AB*] *Neptunes* best *C+:*   armes *A–G Gros.*]
    arme *H*

XLV *A*] XLIX *B–E* LI *F–H* LIIII *Gros.*
  4 cares] care *H*
  9 th'ymagery of our *AB*] th'imag'ry of our *C* th'imaginary
    of our *DE* th'Images of *F–H*

XLVI *A*] L *B–E* LII *F–H* LV *Gros.*
  5 thee *AB*] thee, *C+:* eyes, *ABF–H*] eyes. *C–E*
 13 they shall discouer *A–E*] in them appeare *F+*
 14 was thy louer *A–E*] lou'd thee deare *F+*

XLVI] *after this sonnet C–E have as* LI, *F–H as* LIII, *Gros. as*
  LVI:

A S to the Roman that would free his Land,
  His error was his honour and renowne:
And more the fame of his mistaking hand,
Then if he had the Tyrant ouer-throwne.
So DELIA, hath mine errour made me knowne.
  And my deceiu'd attempt, deseru'd more fame,
  Then if I had the victory mine owne:
  And thy hard hart had yeelded vp the same.

And so likewise, renowmed is thy blame,
Thy crueltie, thy glorie; ô strange case,   (10)
That errours should be grac'd that merrite shame,
And sinne of frownes bring honor to the face.
Yet happy DELIA that thou wast vnkind,
But happier yet, if thou wouldst change thy minde.

(5) DELIA, *F–H*] DELIA *C–E*
(14) But happier yet *C–E*] Though happier far *F–H*

XLVII *A*] LI *B* LII *C–E* LIIII *F–H* LVII *Gros.; it appears also
in John Daniel's Songs, 1606*
   1   that ioyes *A–E*] delights *F–H Songs*
   8   giue] giues *Songs*
9–12] *lines 9–10 follow 11–12 Songs*
  13 O happie ground that makes *A–E*] For no ground els
could make *F–H Songs*
  14 And blessed hand that giues *A–E*] Nor other hand could
giue *F–H Songs* (other *misprinted* o her *G*): sweete *A–
E Songs*] true *F–H*

XLVIII *A*] LII *B* LIII *C–E* LV *F–H* LVIII *Gros.*
   1   vnambitious] ambitious *G*
   9   nor[1]] not *Gros.*
  11 rich *AB Gros.*] poore *C–H:* though *AB Gros.*] and
C–H
  14 *A–E*] No other prouder Brookes shall heare my wrong.
F+

XLIX *A*] LIII *B* LIIII *C–E* LVI *F–H* LIX *Gros.*
   1   papers *A–E*] lines *F+*
   2   desiers *AB*] desires *C–E* desire *F–H*
   3   desiers *A*] desires *B–E* desire *F–H:* the euer burning
tapers *A–E*] which from darke sorrow shines *F+*
   4   fiers *AB*] fires *C–E* fire *F–H*
   5   fiers *AB*] fires *C–E* fire *F–H*
   6   *A–E*] Which pittie not the wounds made by their might,
F–H their (*for the FH*) *G*
   7   In humble *A–E*] Shew'd in these *F+*
   8   I offer *A–E*] here offred *F+*
   9   sith she scornes her owne *A–E*] since she weighs them
not *F+*
  13 selfe *A–E*] Muse *F+*

L *A*] appears as Sonnet 25 in New. LIIII *B* LV *C–E* LVII *F–H*
LX *Gros.*

1 Loe heere *A–E*] Lo here *F–H* To heare *New.:*   vnfaining *A–E*] entire *F–H* not faining *New.*

2 That loue hath paide *A–E*] Which loue doth pay *F–H*
That dutie paies *New.:*   extorted *A–E*] extorts *F–H*
extorteth *New.*

3 Beholde] These beare *New.:*   my iust complayning *A–
E*] a chast desire *F–H* my wofull paining *New.*

4 That shewes *A–E*] Which tells *F–H:*   imported *A–E*]
imports *F–H*

4] These Oliue braunches mercie still exorteth. *New.*

5 plaintes fraught with desire *A–E*] passions, beauties due
F–H plaints with chast desires *New.*

7 hopes aspire *A–E*] soule aspires *New.*

7] That Crueltie her selfe might grieue to view *F–H*

8 mine *A–E*] my *New.*

8] Th'affliction her vnkind disdaine doth moue. *F–H*

9 *A–E*] And how I liue cast down from off all myrth, *F–H*
Wherein (poore soule) I liue exil'd from mirth, *New.*

10 none but despayre about mee *A–E New.*] onely but with
Dispaire *F–H*

11 abortiue, perisht at *A–E*] abortiue, perish in *F–H* liberties perisht in *New.* (*Gros. in a note accepts* perisht)

12 cares *B–E*] carres *A* griefs *F–H* care's *New.:*   will not
dye without mee *A–E New.*] care succeeding care *F–H*

13–14] What shall I doo but sigh and waile, the while
My martyrdome exceedes the highest stile. *New.*

FINIS. A–E] om. *F–H New.*

The Ode *is followed in F+ by* A Pastorall ('O Happy
golden Age'). *They are found also, with* Rosamond, *in*
Certaine Small Poems, 1605, *and* Certaine Small Workes,
1607 *and* 1611, *in these three instances accompanied by*
Ulisses and the Syren. *The 1611 volume thus contains the*
Ode *and* Pastorall *twice: first after* Rosamond, *then after*
Delia. *Editions of the* Ode *are referred to as follows:*

A	Delia,	1592 (*Pforzheimer*)
B	*Ditto*	1592 (*Widener*)
C	*Ditto*	1594 (*Widener*)
D	*Ditto*	1595 (*Huntington*)
E	*Ditto*	1598 (*British Museum*)

F   *Ditto*   1601, 1602 (*Harvard*)
G   ROSAMOND, 1605 (*Harvard*)
H   *Ditto*   1607 (*British Museum*)
I^1 *Ditto*
I^2 DELIA, } 1611 (*Harvard*)
K   *Ditto*   1623 (*Harvard*)
  Gros. GROSART'S *ed. I, 259–260.*

Ode, 2 Passing *AB*] passing *C* + *and so with ll. 4, 6, etc.*
   3 vnto] to *A*
  20 true *A* Gros.] *om.* B–K
  22 depended] dependeth I^1

The four poems which follow appeared in New., Sonnets 3, 10, 12, 16, and are presumably Daniel's though never reprinted by him. Gros. gives the last three (I, 27, 28) and the first quatrain of 'The onely bird' (I, 25–26) which he completed, however, having turned two leaves, with the last ten lines of Sonnet 7, our XIII, 'For haples loe,' ff.

(i)

THe onely bird alone that Nature frames,
   When weary of the tedious life shee liues,
By fier dies, yet finds new life in flames,
Hir ashes to hir shape new essence giues.

When onely I the onely wretched wight,
Wearie of life that breaths but sorrows blasts,
Pursues the flame of such a beautie bright,
That burnes my heart, and yet my life still lasts.

O Soueraigne light that with thy sacred flame
Consumes my life, reuiue me after this,   10
And make me (with the happie bird) the same
That dies to liue, by fauour of thy blisse.
   This deede of thine shall shew a Goddesse power,
   In so long death, to grant one liuing hower.

(ii)

THe slie Inchanter, when to worke his will
   And secret wrong on some forespoken wight,
Frames waxe, in forme to represent aright

The poore vnwitting wretch he meanes to kill,
And prickes the image, fram'd by Magicks skill;
Whereby to vexe the partie day and night:
Like hath she done, whose shew bewitcht my sight
To beauties charmes, her Louers bloud to spill.

For first, like waxe she fram'd me by her eyes,
Whose rayes sharp poynted set vpon my brest,   10
Martyres my life, and plagues me in this wise
With lingring paine to perish in vnrest;
Naught could (saue this) my sweetest faire suffice
    To trie her arte on him that loues her best.

(iii)

THe tablet of my heauie fortunes heere
    Vpon thine Altare (*Paphian* Power) I place;
The greeuous shipwracke of my trauels deere
In bulged barke, all perisht in disgrace.

That traitor Loue, was Pilot to my woe,
My Sailes were hope, spread with my sighs of griefe,
The twinelights which my haples course did show,
Hard by th'inconstant sands of false reliefe,

Were two bright starres which led my view apart,
A Sirens voice allur'd me come so neare,   10
To perish on the marble of her hart,
A danger which my soule did neuer feare:
    Lo thus he fares that trusts a calme too much;
    And thus fare I whose credit hath beene such.

(iv)

WAy but the cause, and giue me leaue to plaine me,
    For all my hurt, that my harts Queene hath wrought it,
Shee whom I loue so deare, the more to paine me,
Withholds my right, where I haue dearely bought it.

Dearely I bought that was so highly rated,
Euen with the price of bloud and bodies wasting,
Shee would not yeeld that ought might be abated,
For all shee saw my Loue was pure and lasting.

And yet now scornes performance of the passion,
And with hir presence Iustice ouerruleth,   10
Shee tels me flat hir beauty beares no action,
And so my plee and proces shee excludeth:
    What wrong shee doth, the world may well perceiue it,
    To accept my faith at first, and then to leaue it.

(ii)   10 rayes *Gros*.] nayes *New*.
       11 in *New*.] on *Gros*.

(iii) 6 hope *New*.] loose *Gros*.
       9 Were *Ed*.] Where *New*. *Gros*.

(iv)   14 my *New*.] of *Gros*.

THE COMPLAINT OF ROSAMOND

Editions are referred to as follows:

A DELIA *and* ROSAMOND (*first edition*), 1592 (*Widener*)
B   *Ditto*   (*second edition*), 1592 (*Bodleian*)
C DELIA AND ROSAMOND AUGMENTED, 1594 (*Widener*)
D   *Ditto*   1595 (*Huntington*)
E [*Ditto*   1598] (*British Museum*)
F POETICALL ESSAYES,   1599 (*British Museum*)
G WORKS,   1601, 1602 (*Harvard*)
H CERTAINE SMALL POEMS,   1605 (*Harvard*)
I   CERTAINE SMALL WORKES, 1607 (*British Museum*)
K   *Ditto*   1611 (*Harvard*)
L WHOLE WORKES,   1623 (*Harvard*)

Gros. GROSART'S *ed., I, 81–113, recorded only as it differs from L.*

Many important revisions occur in C, F, G, and H, and there are a few in I. For what used to be regarded as the third issue of Rosamond, *actually the F text, see Sellers's* Bibliography, *p. 33.*

  1   from *A–HL*] of *IK*
 11   The euer *F*+] Th'euer *A–E*
 13   that *A*] the *B*+
 16   this] the *K*
 25   *Shores*] Shores *A*
 30   Whilome] *Whilome A*
 33   Comes] Come *E:*   since] whilst *L*
 37   th'affliction *A–K Gros.*] th'affection *L*
 38   hath] haue *K*
 41   Thy] The *L:*   depending] depend *K*
 43   deygne *B*+] deynge *A*
 44   sigh] sighs *L*
 84   hap *A–CEFH–K*] hope *GL*
 97   Ah *A–CEFL*] Ay *G–K:*   this *A–CEFL*] that *G–K* (*for variant readings in different copies of G, see p. 168, above*)
 98   *after this line G*+ *add the following:*

There whereas fraile and tender Beuty stands,
With all assaulting powres inuironed;
Hauing but prayers and weake feeble hands

To hold their honors Fort vnvanquished;
There where to stand, and be vnconquered,
　Is to b'aboue the nature of our kinde,
　That cannot long for pittie be vnkinde.

(3)　prayers and weake *GHL*] onely praiers and *IK*
(5)　where *GHL*] were *IK*

104　Soone *A–CEFH+*] Some *G:*　tyrannize, *BCE+*] tyran-
　　nize. *A*
129　women *A–HL*] woman *IK*
132　her with her proper fayre *A–E*] them in their best at-
　　tires *F+*
133　*A–E*] Of youth and beautie which the world admires.
　　F+
136　The *AB*] That *C+:*　new-found shame *C+*] newfound-
　　shame *AB*
147　honors *AB*] honour *C+*
154　the] *om. K:*　that *A*] which *B+:*　mine] my *F*
161　hath *A*] had *B+*
162　*Fraunce Ed.*] Fraunce *AB capitals or italics C+*
163　*A–E*] And all the triumphes of his honor wun: *F+*
165　bosome breedes *A–E*] brest begun *F+*
166　feedes *A–E*] drew on *F+*
167　chastity] chastitiy *A:*　opposes *A–E*] contends *F+*
168　*A–E*] With force of honour, which my shame defends.
　　F+
172　should *A–HL*] would *IK*
173　But] Bnt *A*
177　a state *AB*] estate *C+*
179　pleasures *A–CF+*] pleasure *DE*
184　some] same *K*
185　th'incompatible *A–GL*] th'incomparible *HI* th'incom-
　　parable *K*
199　forget *A–HL*] to forget *IK*
214　like *A–GL*] our *H–K*
220　The one *E*] Th'one *A–DF+*
223　may *A–E*] might *F+*
225　saith *AB*] said *C+*
237–238] *not indented in A*
243　what] that *E*
264　*A–GL*] Ages opinion, Customes out-worne fashion, *H–K*
271　vnworthy *ABK*] vnworthy, *C–IL*

(195)

272 blasts *AB*] blast *C*+
284 the *AB*] thy *C*+ (*with some hesitation I retain the earlier
     reading, cf. 136, 681*)
287 sees *A Gros.*] see *B–L:* our *A–HL*] the *IK*
288–294 *A–H Gros.*] om. *I–L*
293 not *A–CF–H Gros.*] now *DE*
298 the *AB*] om. *C*+
300 impression] impressions *E*
304 Seeing my youth *A–GL*] See'ing my weake youth *H–K*
311 euen in *B–GL*] in *A* euen vpon *HI* euer vpon *K*
314 can *AB*] gan *C*+
316 thy *A–HL*] the *IK*
325 Serpent] Sathan *K*
366 attend *C*+] attend: *AB*
368 long-desired work *Ed.*] long desired-work *AB* long-
     desired worke *C*+
375 work-mans *A–GL*] worke-mens *H–K*
383 Beating *A–K Gros.*] Bathing *L*
394 O] om. *K*
397 eyes] om. *A*
399 that *AB*] which *C*+
401 found *AB*] finde *C*+
424 had I not] had I had not *A:* powre for *A–GL*] vertue
     H–K
426 vs *AB*] om. *C*+
427 vs *AB*] om. *C*+
434 sports] sport *L*
438 no] to *K:* mutuall] naturall *L*
441 to come] to co come *A*
442 receiu'd *A–CE–HL*] reuiu'd *IK*
475 To entertaine *E*] T'entertaine *A–CF*+
476 Fuell *A–CE–IL*] Euill *K:* flames *A–CE–GL*] fiame *H*
     flame *I* frame *K*
479 fortune, and the worlds *A–CE–GL*] misfortune th'ages
     H misfortune, th'ages *I* misfortune, the ages *K*
484 enuy' *A–CE–GL*] Hate *H–K*
492 Conducting *ABE*] Condemning (*corrected in Errata*) *C*
     Condemning *F*+
493 *Argos A*] *Argus BCE*+ (*probably Daniel wrote Argus*)
498 through] though *E*
508 vnlesse] if not *L*
512 Nature] Mature *I*

517   in this vse their dehorting *ABDE*] (in this) vse their de-
      horting *C* from this, do vs dehort *F*+
518   resorting *A–E*] resort *F*+
519   Witnes] Witnest *A*
520   wondrous] wonrdous *A*
521   women *A–CF*] woman *DEG*+
542   She's] Sh's *A*
544   sincerely *A–HL*] sinceryty *I* sincerity *K*
556   eyes *ABDE*] eye *CF*+
570   Queene] Qneene *A:*   deale: *AB*] deale, *C*+
583   raging] ranging *L*
585   Furiously assaults *A–GL*] Doth furiously assault *H–K*
593   would] could *L*
595   For no beast *A–E*] No beast being *F*+
595] *after this line C+ add the following:*

Heere take (saith shee) thou impudent vncleane,
Base graceles strumpet, take this next your hart;
Your loue-sick hart, that ouer-charg'd hath beene
With pleasures surfeite, must be purg'd with arte.
This potion hath a power, that will conuart
   To nought those humors that oppresse you so.
   And (Gerle,) Ile see you take it ere I goe.

What stand you now amaz'd, retire you back?
Tremble you (minion?) come dispatch with speed.
There is no helpe, your Champion now you lack,   (10)
And all these teares you shed will nothing steed;
Those dainty fingers needes must doe the deed.
   Take it, or I will drench you els by force,
   And trifle not, least that I vse you worse.

Hauing this bloody doome from hellish breath,
My wofull eyes on euery side I cast:
Rigor about me, in my hand my death,
Presenting mee the horror of my last;
All hope of pitty and of comfort past.
   No meanes, no powre, no forces to contend,   (20)
   My trembling hands must giue my selfe my end.

597   Must now *AB*] They must *C*+
600   lusts *AB*] lust *C*+
602] *after this line C+ add the following:*

And shee no sooner saw I had it taken,
But foorth shee rushes, (proude with victory,)
And leaues m'alone, of all the world forsaken,
Except of Death, which shee had left with me.
(Death and my selfe alone together be.)
 To whom shee did her full reuenge refer.
 Ah poore weake conquest both for him and her.

Then straight my Conscience summons vp my sin,
T'appeare before me, in a hideous face;
Now doth the terror of my soule begin,   (10)
When eu'ry corner of that hatefull place
Dectates mine error, and reueales disgrace;
 Whilst I remaine opprest in euery part,
 Death in my bodie, horror at my hart.

Downe on my bed my lothsome selfe I cast,
The bed that likewise giues in euidence
Against my soule, and tells I was vnchast,
Tells I was wanton, tells I followed sence.
And therefore cast, by guilt of mine offence,
 Must heere the right of heauen needes satis-fie. (20)
 And where I wanton lay, must wretched die.

Heere I began to waile my hard mishap,
My suddaine, strange vnlookt for misery.
Accusing them that did my youth intrap,
To gyue me such a fall of infamie.
And poore distressed ROSAMOND, (said I,)
 Is this thy glory got, to die forlorne
 In Dezarts, where no eare can heare thee morne?

Nor any eye of pitty to behold
The wofull end of thy sad tragedie;   (30)
But that thy wrongs vnseene, thy tale vntold,
Must heere in secrete silence buried lie.
And with thee, thine excuse together die.
 Thy sin reueal'd, but thy repentance hid,
 Thy shame aliue, but dead what thy death did.

Yet breathe out to these walls the breath of mone,
Tell th'ayre thy plaints, sith men thou canst not tell.
And though thou perrish desolate alone,
Tell yet thy selfe, what thy selfe knowes too well:

Vtter thy griefe where-with thy soule doth swell.　　(40)
　　And let thy hart, pitty thy harts remorse,
　　And be thy selfe the mourner and the Corse.

Condole thee heere, clad all in black dispaire,
With silence onely, and a dying bed;
Thou that of late, so florishing, so fayre,
Did glorious liue, admir'd and honored:
And now from friends, from succour hether led,
　　Art made a spoyle to lust, to wrath, to death,
　　And in disgrace, forst heere to yeeld thy breath.

Did Nature (ô for thys) deliberate,　　(50)
To shew in thee the glory of her best;
Framing thine eye the star of thy ill fate,
And made thy face the foe to spoyle the rest?
O Beautie, thou an enemy profest,
　　To chastitie and vs that loue thee most,
　　Without thee how w'are loath'd, & w̆ thee lost?

O you that proude with liberty and beautie,
(And ô may well be proude that you be so,)
Glitter in Court, lou'd and obseru'd of dutie;
O that I might to you but ere I goe　　(60)
Speake what I feele, to warne you by my woe,
　　To keepe your feet in pure cleane pathes of shame,
　　That no inticing may diuert the same.

See'ng how against your tender weaknes still,
The strength of wit, of gold, and all is bent;
And all th'assaults that euer might or skill,
Can giue against a chaste and cleane intent:
Ah let not greatnes worke you to consent.
　　The spot is foule, though by a Monarch made,
　　Kings cannot priuiledge a sinne forbade.　　(70)

Lock vp therefore the treasure of your loue,
Vnder the surest keyes of feare and shame:
And let no powres haue powre chast thoughts to moue
To make a lawlesse entry on your fame.
Open to those the comfort of your flame,
　　Whose equall loue shal martch with equal pace,
　　In those pure waies that leade to no disgrace.

For see how many discontented beds,
Our owne aspyring, or our Parents pride
Haue caus'd, whilst that ambition vainely weds   (80)
Wealth and not loue, honor and nought beside:
Whilst married but to titles, we abide
    As wedded widdowes, wanting what we haue,
    When shadowes cannot giue vs what we craue.

Or whilst we spend the freshest of our time,
The sweet of youth in plotting in the ayre;
Alas how oft wee fall, hoping to clime.
Or wither as vnprofitably faire,
Whilst those decayes which are without repayre,
    Make vs neglected, scorned and reprou'd.   (90)
    (And ô what are we, if we be not lou'd?)

Fasten therefore vpon occasions fit,
Least this, or that, or like disgrace as mine,
Doe ouer-take your youth to ruine it,
And clowde with infamie your beauties shine:
Seeing how many seeke to vndermine
    The treasury that's vnpossest of any:
    And hard tis kept that is desir'd of many.

And flye, (ô flye,) these Bed-brokers vncleane,
(The Monsters of our sexe,) that make a pray   (100)
Of theyr owne kind, by an vnkindly meane;
And euen (like Vipers,) eating out a way
Th'row th'wombe of their own shame, accursed they
    Lyue by the death of Fame, the gaine of sin,
    The filth of lust, vncleanes wallowes in.

O is it not enough that wee, (poore wee,)
Haue weaknes, beauty, gold, and men our foes,
But we must haue some of our selues to bee
Traytors vnto our selues, to ioyne with those?
Such as our feeble forces doe disclose,   (110)
    And still betray our cause, our shame, our youth,
    To lust, to follie, and to mens vntruth?

Hatefull confounders both of blood and lawes,
Vilde Orators of shame, that pleade delight:
Vngracious Agents in a wicked cause,
Factors for darknes, messengers of night,

Serpents of guile, diuels, that doe inuite
The wanton taste of that forbidden tree,
Whose fruit once pluckt, will shew how foule we be.

You in the habite of a graue aspect, (120)
(In credite by the trust of yeeres,) can shoe
The cunning wayes of lust, and can direct
The fayre and wilie wantons how to goe:
Hauing (your lothsome selues) your youth spent so.
And in vncleanes, euer haue beene fed,
By the reuenue of a wanton bed.

By you, haue beene the innocent betrayd,
The blushing fearefull boldned vnto sin,
The wife made subtile, subtile made the mayd,
The husband scorn'd, dishonored the kin: (130)
Parents disgrac'd, children infamous been.
Confus'd our race, and falsi-fied our blood,
Whilst fathers sonnes, possess wrong Fathers good.

This, and much more, I would haue vttred then,
A testament to be recorded still,
Signd with my blood, subscrib'd with Conscience pen,
To warne the faire and beautifull from ill.
And ô I wish (by th'example of my will,)
I had not left this sin vnto the fayre,
But dyde intestat to haue had no heire. (140)

(7)   Ah $C-E$] Oh $F+$
(30) thy $CF-K$] my DEL
(37) sith $C-E$] since $F+$
(46) Did $C-F$] Didst $G+$
(50) (ô for thys) deliberate $C-F$] (for this good) ingeniate $G+$
(53) And made $C-F$] Making $G+$
(56) thee² $C-IL$] the K
(57) O $C-F$] You, $G+$
(58) ô may well $C-F$] well may you $G+$
(60) O that $C-F$] Would God $G+$
(62) pure cleane $C-F$] cleanly $G+$
(65) of² $C-K$] and L
(70) a sinne $C-F$] what God $G+$
(83) what $C-IL$] that K
(88) wither $C-FH$] whither $GI+$
(94) to $C-K$] or L
(97) The treasury CD] The treasurie $E-IL$ Treasurie K
(103) Th'row F] Thorow $C-E$ Through GHL Throgh IK
(105) wallowes $C-IL$] swallowes K

(106) O is it $C-F$] As if t'were $G+$
(119) Whose $D+$] whose C
(123) to $C-GL$] they $H-K$
(124) your[1] $C-GL$] youth $H-K$
(138) And ô I $C-F$] Though I could $G+$
(139) sin $C-F$] note $G+$

603 The poyson soone disperc'd AB] But now, the poyson
    spred $C+$
604 Had dispossess'd AB] Gan dispossesse $C+$
605 When AB] And $C+$:   respecting death, the last of
    paines, $Ed.$] respecting, death the last of paines, AB re-
    specting Death, (the last of paines,) $C+$ (*with minor
    variations*)
606 th'ensigne $C+$ the'nsigne AB
616 beene] be K
621 feeles that hart, $B-DF+$] feeles, that hart A feeles that
    hart E
623 aright $C-E$] a right AB
623] That ouerwhelms vs, or confounds vs quite? $F+$ (F
    misprints ouerwhemls)
624 nor[1]] not K
627 affects] effects K
630 cares] care D: griefes] griefe, B
631 a way $C+$] away AB
649 inflicted] afflicted A
656 hath] haue E
664 euen $A-GL$] now euen $H-K$
666 quoth AB] saith $C+$
669 sorrowing $A-HL$] for owing IK
679 it] her K
681 The[1] AB] These $C+$
690 women kind $A-GKL$] woman kinde HI
697 that AB] hee $C+$:   might AB] should $C+$
699 knowes ABL] knew $C-K$
713 esteem'd so] esteemed K
714 The $A-GL$] Our $H-K$
720 renewd, my fame $C+$] renewd by fame, AB
729 thee $A-F$] *om.* $G+$
731 thee $A-F$] *om.* $G+$
732 sigh $A-GL$] sight $H-K$ (*cf. line 44, above*)
736 vanisht $ABDEK$ $Gros.$] vanquisht $CF-IL$
739 ah $A-F$] yet $G+$

MUSOPHILUS

Editions are referred to as follows:
  A Poeticall Essayes, 1599 (*Harvard*)
  B Works, 1601, 1602 (*Harvard*)
  C Certaine Small Workes, 1607 (*British Museum*)
  D *Ditto* 1611 (*Harvard*)
  E Whole Workes, 1623 (*Harvard*)
  Gros. Grosart's *ed., I, 223–256, recorded only as it differs from E. C represents a pretty complete revision by the poet, while E (which derives from B) contains an unusual number of misprints, duly reproduced for the most part in Gros. Lines 995 ff. are found only in A.*

To Fulke Greuill, 1–17 *ABE*] om. *CD*

  10 Here *A*] Where *BE*

In D this dedicatory sonnet is replaced by the lines printed below. They appear also, with some slight variations in spelling, etc., in the curious B.M. copy of C, 644. a. 41., occupying one of several extra leaves near the beginning of the volume. On recto of the leaf preceding is: 'Musophilus/Or/A Defence Of/Poesie./Carmen amat quisquis carmine digna gerit', *with the ornament of CD. In this copy, which is fully described by Mr. Sellers, the two leaves, N4–N5, just before the* Musophilus *text, are wanting: but N4 should have borne, recto and verso, the concluding stanzas of* Ulisses *and the* Syren, *and* N5, *the t.p., leaving no room for the lines to Grevill. (The W. A. White copy, seen by me since the above was written, has the second dedication, again as an after-thought, at the beginning of the volume. It has also N4–N5, which are quite as expected.)*

TO THE RIGHT
worthy Knight Sir
Fovlke Grivell.

I F I haue err'd or run a course vnfit
  To vent my vnderstanding in this kinde
Your approbation hath beene cause of it
That fed this gratefull error of my mind

For your most worthy and iudicious Knight
Did first draw forth from close obscuritie
My vnpresuming verse into the light   (10)
And grac'd the same, & made me known therby:
And euery man we see is easily
Confirm'd in that wherein he takes delight,
But chiefly when he findes his industry
Allow'd by him he knowes can iudge aright.
Though praise I feare me is not vertues friend
So much as we would make it seeme to be,
For more vndone, then raised thereby we see
Whereas themselues men cannot comprehend.
And for my part, I haue beene oft constraind   (20)
To reexamine this my course herein
And question with my selfe what is contained
Or what solidity there was therein.
And then in casting it with that account
And recknings of the world, I therein found
It came farre short, and neither did amount
In valew with those hopes I did propound
Nor answer'd the expences of my time
Which made me much distrust my selfe & ryme.
    And I was flying from my heart and from   (30)
The station I was set in, to remaine:
And had left all, had not fresh forces come
And brought me backe vnto my selfe againe,
And furnisht my distrusts with this defence
This armor wherewith all the best I could
I haue made good, against the difference
Of fortune, and the world, that which I told.
    And haue maintain'd your honor in the same
    Who herein holds an interest in my fame.

SAMVELL DANIELL.

 (3) GRIVELL *Ed.*] GKIVELL *D*
(29) *ryme.* *Ed.*] *ryme D*
 10   when] then *D*
 16] *projects in A*
 27   A gaine *Ed.*] Againe *A* Againe, *BE* A Gaine *CD*
 42   other] others *D*
 43   *Philocosmus.*] *Philocosmus, A*
 58   it] *om. Gros.*
 60   learning] learned *D*

63   Whose *ABE*] As *CD*
67   strings] string *E*
77   now *CD*] new *ABE*
83   Nature and *ABE*] Times, and to *CD*
91   contemptible *CD*] contemptiblie *A* contemptibly *BE*
93   right-deseruing *AB*] right deseruing *CD* right-disceruing
      E right-discerning *Gros.*
94   of confusion *ABE*] that confused ill *CD*
95   that *ABE*] which *CD*
96   imitation *ABE*] imitation still *CD*
98]   *after this line CD have:*
      Nor what he ought to doe but what is done.
107   cōfounds, *Ed.*] cōfounds *A* confounds, *B+*
111   Gath'ring, incroching *ABE*] Incroching, gathering *CD*
119   iniquitie, *CD*] iniquitie. *A* Iniquitie, *BE* Iniquitie: *Gros.*
144   libertie: *D*] libertie? *A* Libertie: *BE* liberty: *C*
149–150] *these lines are reversed in B and corrected in some*
      copies by means of a cancel slip pasted loosely over them
150   vanished] vanquished *D*
152   last. *BE*] last *A* last, *CD*
157   rime] time *D*
161   threatning *ABE*] threatnings *CD*
167   in the withering *ABE*] the diflorishing *C* the deflourish-
      ing *D*
174   spring] springing *E*
187   sympathize *ABE*] simpathize *C* simpathizes *D*
196   earth *ABE*] world *CD*
202   shame,] shame *A*
211   fortunately] so fortunately *B*
215–228 *ABE*] *om. CD*
228   small *AE*] *om. B*
232   condemne] contemne *D*
234   vertues] vertue *D*
239   Knowing *ABE*] Seeing how *CD*
246   a] an *E*
254   with all *ABE*] withall *CD*
256   in generall] ingenerall *A*
258   to] no *D*
262   in] to *D*
272   neglected] neglect *D*
289   vnhallowed *A–D Gros.*] vnhollowed *E*
301   and] all *E*

(205)

306 Thee] The *E*

307 Either truth, goodnes, vertue *ABE*] And either truth and goodnes *CD*

310 vpon,] vpon *A*

316 onely *ACD*] *om. BE*

323 accessary *ABE*] aceessaries *C* accessaries *D*

325 names *A*] name *BCE* nan e (Name *Errata*) *D*

330 truer] true *D*

331–334 *ABE*] *om. CD*

335 honors *ABE*] reliques *CD*: ill defend *ABE*] neuer crowne *CD*

336 that *ABE*] which *CD*

337 And whereto serue that *ABE*] Witnesse that huge & *CD*

338 That *ABE*] Which *CD*: goodly] godly *A*: plaine *ABE*] plaines *CD*

340 it] he *D*

342 pride *ABE*] power *CD*

343–390 *ABE*] *om. CD*

360 hand *AB*] hands *E*

364 parle *A*] parlee *BE*

391 *ABE*] When in a lesser roome securely lie, *CD*

392 yet lie *ABE*] lie most *CD*

394 thee *ABE*] vs *CD*

408 Striuing to make his *ABE*] And striuing t'haue hir *C* And striuing t'haue her *D*

413 his² *ACD*] *om. BE*

430 is this all *ACD*] in this All, *BE*

439 labors *A–C*] labours *D* labour *E*

440 heard *ABE*] weigh *CD*

443 *ABE*] By following onely what the season brookes, *CD*

446 you not *ABE*] not you *CD*: *Rymes ACD*] and Rymes *BE*

451 ioin'd. *Ed.*] ioin'd *ACD* ioyn'd. *BE*

455 them] then *D*

464 these *BE*] these, *ACD*: they, *BE*] they *ACD*

469 cauilling: *AC*] cauilling *B* cauelling, *D* cauelling *E*

470 Disgrace *ACD*] Disgrace, *BE*: deuise, *ACD*] deuise: *BE*

478 For *ABE*] And *CD*: neither] neuer *D*

488 require *ABE*] requires *CD*

492 doubt, *BE*] doubt *ACD* doubt; *Gros.*

495 naturall] natur all *A*

499　your] our *D*
504　swellings *A–C*] swelling *DE*
544　What, *BE*] What *ACD:*　　then *ACD*] *om. BE*
548　scorne *ABE*] scornes *CD*
556　is] in *D*
557　Doth] Doe *E*
558　*Gros.*] *projects in A–E*
560　but vp *ACD*] vp but *BE*
561　serue] serues *E:*　　others] other *D*
572　That *ABE*] Who *CD*
585　Virtue *AB*] *opposite 587 C printed vertically opposite 587–*
　　　590 D om. E:　　that[1]] not *D*
587　hath] haue *D*
609　*Ed.*] *projects in A+*
611　*Ed.*] *does not project in A+*
625　wherewithall] wherewith all *D*
628　themselues] themselus *A*
634　beast] best *E*
638　heats *ACD*] harts *B* hearts *E*
646　vnhalloweth] vnholloweth *A*
663　But *ABE*] Yet *CD*
671　*ABE*] Whereby we haue bewraide our gouernment *CD*
674　That *ABE*] Which *CD*
677–790　*ABE*] *om. CD*
710] *this line and every third line to 884 project in AB*
711　the other *Ed.*] th'other *ABE*
728] *this line and every third line to 884 project in E, normalized*
　　　by Gros. except at 800
738　tempering *A*] temp'ring *BE* tamp'ring *Gros.*
749　ô *A*] do *BE*
754　Whereon *BE*] where on *A*
762　thrusting *Ed.*] thursting *A* thirsting *BE*
772　hands *AB*] hand *E*
784　roome *AB*] roomes *E*
791　This makes indeed our *ABE*] Nor would our so great *CD*
792　which if dealt aright *A*] which, if dealt aright, *BE*
　　　where (*qy.* were?) they delt aright. *CD*
793　Would *ABE*] But *CD:*　　roome *ABE*] meanes *CD*
804　heritage] heritages *D*
806] *this line and every third line to 884 project in CD*
806　call'd *ABE*] cald *C* clad *D*
807　b'asham'd *ABE*] basham'd *C* be sham'd *D*

808 And stay'ng *ABE*] Who in *CD*
813 disincourag'd] discourag'd *E*
814 wauering] wandring *D*
815 Caring not *ABE*] Not caring *CD*
822 spirits] spirit *E*
826 pillers *AE*] Pillers *B* pillar *CD*
833 more *ABE*] most *CD*
845 raies, *BE*] raies *ACD*
848 waine *A*] wane *BE* vaine *CD*
861 home-faults] homes faultes *D*
867 turning on *ABE*] present way *CD*
869 opposition *ABE*] opposition shall *CD*
870 *ABE*] With an incountring shocke of strength, disioynt *CD*
871 thereupon *ABE*] there withall *CD*
887] *projects in Gros.*
893] *Gros. makes this line, not 891, project and his arrangement thereafter, except ll. 989–994, is not that of A–E*
924 learnings *ACD*] Learnings *B* Learning *E*
926 wey too *A*] weigh too *BE* way to *CD*
948 *Ed.*] *projects in A–E*
961 worlds] world is *D*
989 *ff.*] *om. CD*
995 *ff.*] *om. B+*

EPISTLES

Editions are referred to as follows:

A Panegyrike *and* Epistles, F° [1603] (*British Museum*)
B Panegyrike, Epistles, Defence of Ryme, 8°, 1603 (*Harvard*)
C Tragedie of Philotas (*etc.*), 1607 (*British Museum*)
D Whole Workes, 1623 (*Harvard*)
Gros. Grosart's *ed.*, I, *191–219, recorded only as it differs from D. For another issue of A with the* Defence of Ryme, *see* Sellers, *pp. 36–37. In this issue, which yields no variants, and in B–D, the* Epistles *are followed by the curious verses headed 'The passion of a distressed man' (etc.), reprinted by Grosart, I, 273–276.*

To Sir Tho: Egerton

14 fastning *CD*] fasting *AB*
62 *Keeper*] Keeper *A*
74 essoines,] essoines; *A*
76 monster, Malice, *CD*] Monster malice *AB*
93 *Ferdinand king of Castile AB Gros.*] *om. CD*
102 *The king of Hungarie AB Gros.*] *om. CD*
107 *Difficultatem facit doctrina AB Gros.*] *om. CD*
135 iudgements] iudgement *D*
137 surly *A*] surely *B–D: Law*] Law *A*
139 innocencie *AB*] innocencies *CD*
150 *Necessitas est lex temporum AB*] *om. CD Necessitas est lex temporis Gros.*
178 *A remedie for defending ill causes AB Gros.*] *om. CD*
198 hand, *CD*] hand; *AB*

To the Lord Henry Howard

7   Nor *A–C Gros.*] Not *D*
35 builded *A*] blinded *B–D*
63 turne *A*] runne *B–D*

To the Covntesse of Cvmberland

3] *the title is redivided as in D,* Cvm/berland *A*
14 these] the *D*

(209)

A DEFENCE OF RYME

Editions are indicated as follows:

A A PANEGYRIKE CONGRATVLATORY, *etc., F°* [1603] (*Harvard*)
B *Ditto* *8°*, 1603 (*Harvard*)
C THE TRAGEDIE OF PHILOTAS, *etc.*, 1607 (*British Museum*)
Gros. GROSART'S *ed., IV, 31–67, recorded only as it differs from*
C. New paragraphs were introduced, and a few minor revisions
made, in B. A–C have running title 'An Apologie for Ryme.'

To the Louers of Ryme, 18 what] that *C*
15   not] no *Gros.*
22   or *A*] & *BC*
23   receiuing *A*] & receiued *BC*
76   these] those *Gros.*
80   *alienæ*] aliena *Gros.*
83   powerfully] powerfullly *A*
87   indenize] modernize *Gros.*
153 made] make *Gros.*
156 their] the *C*
173 *arbitratores*] arbritratores *A*
193 or] as *Gros.*
195 we are *A*] were *BC*
203 betwixt] betweene *C*
208 accent] accents *A*
213 force *A*] forme *BC*
230 prison] person *Gros.*
230 these] those *Gros.*
231 still] stile *Gros.*
232 a] as *Gros.*
243 *populus leuis*] populis leuit *Gros.*
258 seeme] secure *Gros.*
272 vnto] to *C*
278 possibly] possible *B*
304 were] was *Gros.*
335 not *AB Gros.*] nor *C*
349–50 hit, the certaine close of delight] hit the certein close
         of delight, *C*

356   his] this *C*
378   be but a *A*] but *BC*
395   which well] which being well *C*
398   yet ¹ *A*] om. *BC*
398   spake] speake *Gros.*
399   malediction] maledictions *C*
434   Nor could this *ff. A*] *new paragraph BC*
441   And with *Petrarch ff. A*] *new paragraph BC*
445   *Leonardus Aretinus*] Leonardus, *Aretinus Gros.*
445   *Laurentius BC*] *Laurentins A*
456   Him followed *Bessarion ff. A*] *new paragraph BC*
457   *Theodore A*] *Theodorus BC*
461   then] them *Gros.*
464   When *Pomponius ff. A*] *new paragraph BC*
468   vp *A*] om. *BC*
471   And yet long before *ff. A*] *new paragraph BC*
475   aboue *A*] about *BC*
478   registred: *C*] registred. *AB*
499   We must not looke *ff. A*] *new paragraph BC*
503   syte] sight *C*
511   forecast] forecasts *C*
514   When the best measure *ff. A*] *new paragraph BC*
518   The distribution of giftes *ff. A*] *new paragraph BC*
519   hath] haue *C*
539   seemes] seemeth *C*
541   *parerent*] pararent *Gros.*
542   *perferrent A*] preferrent *BC*
550   that] the *Gros.*
563   There is but one learning *ff. A*] *new paragraph BC*
573   in] on *Gros.*
574   habit *A*] pase *BC*
583   them *A*] it *BC*
583   Let vs go no further *ff. A*] *new paragraph BC*
584   this] the *Gros.*
598   match *AB Gros.*] march *C*
599   But this innouation *ff. A*] *new paragraph BC*
604   is it *A*] it is *BC*
608   me thinkes] wee think *Gros.*
622   *illam A*] illum *BC*
623   But shal we not tend *ff. A*] *new paragraph BC*
633   these] those *Gros.*
643   my] mine *C*

648 And surely mee thinkes *ff. A*] *new paragraph BC*

669 So that it is *ff. A*] *new paragraph BC*

691 no] in *Gros.*

732 other] others *Gros.*

753 Monosillables] Monosyllable *Gros.*

761 Next comes the *Elegiacke ff. A*] *at the beginning of a page; not indented though the preceding sentence ends in the middle of a line showing that a new paragraph was intended B new paragraph C*

763 old *A*] *om. BC*

794 numbers *A Gros.*] number *BC*

797 into *A*] in *BC*

799 Verse, *Ed.*] Verse. *AB* verse, *C* verse — *Gros.*

801–02 *Rendrèd* and *Worthìe A*] *Rèndred* and *Worthy BC*

807 *preserues, C*] *preserues. AB*

820 *Cell: C*] *Cell. AB*

838–39 honor of the dead, wrong to the] *om. A (the omission occurs at the end of sig. H5rº: wrong to / [catchword: the /] the fame) cf. ll. 920 ff.*

842 loose] lesse *A*

873 allarum] all-arme *C*

875 with all *Ed.*] withall *A–C* with the words all *Gros.*

884 awe] aire *Gros.*

890–91 effect. For] effect. for *A*

898 *Latinis, Gros.*] *Latinis. A–C*

899 soule, *Gros.*] soule. *A–C*

940 out] *om. Gros.*

953 without] with *C*

959 a couplet] a-
          couplet *A*

964 my] mine *C*

978 certaine] for certaine *Gros.*

1011 And the more to shew *ff.*] *new paragraph A*

1020–21 displacing our wordes, or inuesting new,] *om. Gros.*

1021 onely *A*] openly *BC*

1022 our] *om. Gros.*

1030 establish *A*] stabish *B* stablish *C*

1032–33 to be] *om. Gros.*

ULISSES AND THE SYREN

Editions are referred to as follows:

A   Certaine Small Poems (*after* Rosamond), 1605 (*Harvard*)
B   Certaine Small Workes (*after* Rosamond), 1607 (*B. M.*)
C   *Ditto*   (*after* Rosamond), 1611 (*B. M.*)
D   Whole Workes (*after* Hymen's Triumph), 1623 (*B. M.*)
Gros. Grosart's *ed., I, 270–272, recorded only as it differs from A.*

  7   in] on *Gros.*
 9–10, *etc.*] *there are no stanzaic divisions in Gros.*
12   me there *Ed.*] with thee *A* + (*emendation by H. C. Beeching,* A Selection from the Poetry of Samuel Daniel and Michael Drayton, *1899, p. 189*)
20   This *AB*] Tis (*corrected in Errata*) *C* Tis *D*
22   molest *A*] molest, *B–D*
23   peace, *A*] peace *B–D:*   beguile *A*] beguile, *B* beguile. *CD*
46   thought] thoughts *Gros.*
47   Are recreated] Are. . . . reuealed [*sic*] *Gros.*
56   wights *B–D*] wights. *A* wights, *Gros.*
60   Spirits] Sports *Gros.*
67   heere *A*] here *B–D* heare *Gros.*

EDITIONS USED *

Syr P. S. His Astrophel and Stella. Wherein the excellence of
sweete Poesie is concluded To the end of which are added, sundry other rare Sonnets of diuers Noblemen and Gentlemen.
Thomas Newman, 4°, 1591.

Delia. Contayning certayne Sonnets: with the complaint of
Rosamond.
I. C. for Simon Waterson, 4°, 1592.

Delia. Containing certaine Sonnets: with the complaynt of
Rosamond.
J. C. for S. Watersonne, 4°, 1592.

Delia and Rosamond augmented. Cleopatra.
Simon Waterson, 16°, 1594.

Delia And Rosamond augmented. Cleopatra.
S. Waterson, 8°, 1595.
In The Huntington Library copy, *Rosamond* wants signatures D7, E1, E8 (t.p.
and our ll.50–105, 442–497).

[Delia and Rosamond augmented. Cleopatra. Peter Short for
Simon Waterson, 1598] 12°.
The B. M. copy wants t.p. and signatures A6, A7, A8, A12, B2 (Sonnets VII–XII,
'XIX–XX' = XVIII–XIX, 'XXIII–XXIIII' = XXII–XXIII).

The Poeticall Essayes Of Sam. Danyel. Newly corrected and
augmented.
P. Short for Simon Waterson, 4°, 1599.
Includes *Rosamond, Musophilus.*

The Works of Samuel Daniel Newly augmented.
Simon Waterson, Fol., 1601 [also 1602].
Includes *Delia, Rosamond, Musophilus.*

A Panegyrike Congratulatorie To The Kings Maiestie. Also certaine Epistles, Fol. [1603].

* For further details, see Sellers, 'A Bibliography of the Works of Samuel
Daniel 1585–1623', *Oxford Bibliographical Society, Proceedings and Papers,*
vol. II, part i, 1927.

(215)

A Panegyrike Congratulatory. . . . Also certaine Epistles. With a Defence of Ryme, heeretofore written, and now published by the Author.
V. S. for Edward Blount, Fol. [1603].

A Panegyrike Congratulatorie. . . . Also Certaine Epistles, With A Defence Of Ryme Heretofore Written, And Now Published By The Author.
Edward Blount, 8°, 1603.

Certaine Small Poems Lately Printed: with the Tragedie of Philotas.
G. Eld for Simon Waterson, 8°, 1605.
Includes *Rosamond, Ulisses and the Syren.*

Songs For The Lute Viol and Voice: Composed by I. Danyel.
T. E. for Thomas Adams, Fol., 1606.
Includes *Delia* XLVII and sonnet after XX.

Certaine Small Workes Heretofore Divulged by Samuel Daniel . . . & now againe by him corrected and augmented.
I. W. for Simon Waterson, 8°, 1607.
Includes *To the Reader, Rosamond, Musophilus, Ulisses and the Syren.*

The Tragedie of Philotas.
Melch. Bradwood for Edw. Blount, 12°, 1607.
Includes *Epistles, Defence of Ryme.*

Certaine Small Workes Heretofore Divulged by Samuel Daniell . . . and now againe by him corrected and augmented.
I. L. for Simon Waterson, 12°, 1611.
Includes *To the Reader, Delia, Rosamond, Musophilus, Ulisses and the Syren.*

The Whole Workes Of Samuel Daniel Esquire in Poetrie.
Nicholas Okes for Simon Waterson, 4°, 1623.
Includes *Delia, Rosamond, Musophilus, Epistles, Ulisses and the Syren.*

DATE DUE